MW01288822

Brenda,

I am really looking forward to getting to know you again and making many friends with you!

Love in Him,

Erin

VALLEY OF THE
SHADOW

ELIZABETH STONE AND ERIN STONE

WESTBOW·
PRESS
A DIVISION OF THOMAS NELSON
& ZONDERVAN

Copyright © 2014 Elizabeth Stone.

All rights reserved. No part of this book may be used or reproduced by any means, graphic, electronic, or mechanical, including photocopying, recording, taping or by any information storage retrieval system without the written permission of the publisher except in the case of brief quotations embodied in critical articles and reviews.

WestBow Press books may be ordered through booksellers or by contacting:

WestBow Press
A Division of Thomas Nelson & Zondervan
1663 Liberty Drive
Bloomington, IN 47403
www.westbowpress.com
1 (866) 928-1240

Because of the dynamic nature of the Internet, any web addresses or links contained in this book may have changed since publication and may no longer be valid. The views expressed in this work are solely those of the author and do not necessarily reflect the views of the publisher, and the publisher hereby disclaims any responsibility for them.

Cover and author photographs were taken by the Rev. Greg Stone.

ISBN: 978-1-4908-1619-7 (sc)
ISBN: 978-1-4908-1618-0 (hc)
ISBN: 978-1-4908-1620-3 (e)

Library of Congress Control Number: 2013921110

Printed in the United States of America.

WestBow Press rev. date: 1/29/2014

Bible verses in this book were taken from the King James Version of the Bible.

Bible verses in this book were taken from the Holy Bible, New International Version®, NIV®. Copyright © 1973, 1978, 1984, 2011 by Biblica, Inc.™ Used by permission of Zondervan. All rights reserved worldwide. www.zondervan.com The "NIV" and "New International Version" are trademarks registered in the United States Patent and Trademark Office by Biblica, Inc.™ All rights reserved.

Bible verses in this book were taken from The Holy Bible, English Standard Version® (ESV®), copyright © 2001 by Crossway, a publishing ministry of Good News Publishers. Used by permission. All rights reserved.

Bible verses in this book were taken from the Revised Standard Version of the Bible, copyright 1952 [2nd edition, 1971] by the Division of Christian Education of the National Council of the Churches of Christ in the United States of America. Used by permission. All rights reserved.

CONTENTS

Glory be to the Father, and to the Son, and to the Holy Spirit.

As it was in the beginning, is now and ever shall be,

world without end,

Amen.

To my beloved husband Greg.

~ Elizabeth

To my family and friends, without whom, I would

not be the woman I am today. Thank you.

~ Erin

PREFACE

If I were to choose a book to write and publish, this would not have been the one. I have in my study, a bag; I call it my "Bag of Dreams," and in it are several ongoing writing projects that I would much sooner publish than this work. Why? Because they are all works of the mind — this one is a work of the heart. Frankly, it goes way too near the bone for comfort.

I cannot say this was difficult to write; the words flowed to my pen. It began with a writing contest, a contest I didn't win, yet I have come to believe that this is a story that needs to be told. There are so many people facing the agony of this particular heartache, and whether they are the victims of a suicide attempt, or the survivors (family and friends), the pain is of the most intense kind. The human heart knows very few traumas that penetrate this deeply.

This is a testimony, a story, our story. It is not a how-to book on recognizing symptoms of depression or suicide or how to treat them. My professional interests have led me into those areas somewhat, and since Erin's attempt I have done quite a bit of research which comes into our story obliquely. There are many and far better books that cover the subject. But this book is rather about grace; it is about how God's grace remade our world.

I owe many debts of gratitude to family and friends. First of all to my beloved husband Greg, who has walked the mountaintops and valleys with me for over thirty years; his love and devotion are constant, his friendship is genuine, his commitment is solid, and his eyes always see me as that twenty-something brunette with no diminished beauty. After salvation, he is the greatest gift God has ever given me. My special thanks to Greg also for lending his photographic talent to our project; our cover is his shot of the Valley of Elah in Israel (where David fought Goliath). He also took over two hundred photos of Erin and me for the author picture, and we found one we both agreed on (Greg liked them all). Then to my children, who are the greatest joys of our lives. I appreciate each one for his or her gifts and uniqueness, but also for letting me share our family story. Joshua, Patrick, John-Mark, Erin, and Rebekah gave their permission to share with alacrity, and have supported me in my new endeavors. Special thanks are also due to my readers and editors: Leah Rolling, Carol Kaufmann, and Gracie Stover. Each one gave me insight and encouragement that moved me on toward publication. Many thanks to the congregations of Bradley and Mount Hope Presbyterian Churches, who gave me space and flexibility to walk this valley while I continued to work full-time, and also loved me through it. I also appreciate all my Facebook friends from camp, from school, from the ladies' Bible study, from extended family, and from my kids' friends who weighed in with encouragement and picture selection.

When I began this journey, I asked my daughter's permission to share our story. When Erin offered to help write the story, and give the firsthand account of her own spiritual journey, I was humbled and honored. That she would share, so transparently, the hurt and misery and recovery of her overdose for the sake of others speaks volumes of her sacrificial compassion. Since that time she has become an effective and vocal advocate for troubled teens and peers, and has spoken at camps and in classrooms challenging others with her story. I am unspeakably grateful for her, for her faith and love that put others before herself, and for all her hard work.

The good news is, and one I have long known intellectually, is that God is most palpably present with us in these times of deepest sorrow. Now I have come to know that experientially. There is no human tragedy or grief that the heart of God has not also felt, there is no place He calls us to go that He has not also gone. Like the woman who comes to the well of Jacob parched and alone, we arrive in our circumstances distressed and wounded, and find the Son of God sitting there ready to quench us and give us eternal life. And somehow it surprises us that He was there all along, knowing we would need Him in our darkest days. Yet that is where we find Jesus, anticipating our desperate arrival with His wellspring of living waters.

My prayer is that this book, this epistle of grace, will bring hope and help and healing to those who are also walking through times of sorrow. God is waiting for us in the valleys, and He has walked every step of them before us. He is able and willing to bring us through, and there is always a way through.

"Yea, though I walk through the valley of the shadow of death, I will fear no evil, for Thou art with me; Thy rod and Thy staff they comfort me. Surely goodness and mercy shall follow me all the days of my life, and I shall dwell in the house of the LORD forever." Psalm 23:4-6 (KJV)

In the service of Christ the King,

Elizabeth Stone

When my mother came to me with this idea, I was thrilled to help write our story. It has helped me to really understand what my family was going through during this time in our lives. I know that I am not the only victim of my actions. It is very difficult for teenagers to understand what their actions will inflict on others. I think that this book helps us to understand both sides of the coin.

I know that we all have pain and we all struggle. It is a part of the human process, but by expressing that pain through healthy means, such as writing, we can learn and grow from it. This book is a source of growth and learning for me. I hope that you will enjoy and perhaps learn something new from it as well.

Thank you for reading.

O Israel, put your hope in the LORD,
for with the LORD is unfailing love
and with him is full redemption.
Psalm 130:7 (NIV)

Erin Stone

Are we healed yet?

It is Thanksgiving eve, the twilight hour. In the chill of the night, with a dusting of snow on the ground, two stealthy figures emerge from my house. Shrouded in darkness, they come to the vehicles, and using the keys, they enter. The interior lights are quickly doused, and the perpetrators hide within. Both sliding doors of the mini-van are quietly opened, leaving them ajar. Windows on our sub-compact are rolled down, and there the two warriors take up their positions. It grows darker and colder, and still they wait, knowing that their ambush is unsuspected and of genius proportions. Eventually, an old red jeep pulls up to the house. Since the driveway is already to capacity with vehicles, it pulls onto the lawn. A tall brown-haired young man emerges with a black cocker spaniel at his heels, and a second young man, with lighter hair and blue eyes, is disgorged from the passenger side. With a war cry unrivaled in history their attackers leap from their positions, this one wearing a sombrero and the other with goggles and a pink karate helmet. The young men know their female siblings are upon them, with a well thought out strategy and the element of surprise. Suddenly the peace of the neighborhood is rent by the sound of electronic automatic weapons, plastic foam darts with rubber tips soar through the air. Ah, curses! One of the weapons jams, resulting in an all out charge. The boys, not in any way cowardly or unprepared, leap to retrieve their own weapons, previously loaded and lying ready on the back seat. For the next hour there is a barrage of darts sometimes hitting, mostly missing, as my adult children tear through my house and yard aiming at each other. These largely innocuous missiles, many of which will lie hidden in couches and behind dressers until the next family gathering, these form one of our traditional reunion rituals. What started as a couple of gag gifts has snowballed into a highly competitive strategic game, and now the grandchildren have become corrupted.

I often wonder, years after the event, if we are healed yet, if we are back to normal. What makes a normal Christian family life? Is it the way we dress, or the particular church we attend? Is it Bible reading and prayer at mealtimes? Is it the absence of certain behaviors and the presence of others? Is it the foods we eat or the way we vote or the music we listen to? And when things go wrong, does that mean we have failed? Have we failed God, have we failed ourselves? Are we no longer worthy of the name of Christian? Is our witness for Christ destroyed? What happens to faith when the unthinkable happens? Where is Christ in the furnace of human tragedy?

I found Erin in the closet, lying on the floor. I had stuck my head in the door to tell her to wake up and take the dog out, but she never appeared. Tired and frustrated that I was again coercing her to take care of what was supposed to be her and her sister's dog, I stormed into her room and grabbed her by the arm to get her up. But her arm flopped down to the floor. She was lying across her half-packed suitcase, the insides of which held not only her clothes but also pools of vomit. That's how I found my precious baby girl; that's how the nightmare began.

What is the worst day of your life? Can you pinpoint it? I can. The worst day of my life was that hot summer morning, the day I became a statistic. When you become a statistic, life is thrown into a tailspin. We tend to quantify life in terms of percentages: 50% divorce rate, 33% of all women contract cancer, approximately 4400 teen suicides every year. But when you experience it, it is no longer this abstract quantity out there, sanitized by impersonal percentages, all of a sudden you **are** the statistic, and it is raw, emotional, and fills every corner of your soul. In the economy of Heaven numbers are not important, but we live in a world that analyzes the tragedies of life. This is my story, the story of my family, when we became a statistic. And it is the story of how God's redeeming love burns brightest in the furnace, how He walks with us in the furnace.

CHAPTER 1

Wholly Family

One of my favorite refrigerator magnets says: "Our family puts the **fun** in dysfunctional." That's good – I might say Godly – family philosophy. We like to think that "happily ever after" is automatic. Two people who love God and love each other come together at a great feast of a family wedding, and it is supposed to be perfect from then on. I, like so many other women and girls, have grown up on the fairy tales and romantic comedies that teach us that the pinnacle of romance is that breathless kiss at the end of the movie, the engagement or the wedding embrace that seals the pledging of troth. Prince Charming is carrying us off into the sunset on his gleaming stallion to a golden palace. In reality, marriage and family life is more like a crazy wild roller coaster ride. Instead of a white horse, we hop onto this brightly painted car with at least one other person, virtually a stranger, and the bars come down and lock us in our seats. Then comes the slow chunka-chunka as the car is grabbed underneath and hauled up that first hill, which seems like it was made just to torture us with anxiety as we watch the ground get further and further away. Then we come to the apex of that first hill, and our brain is screaming, "What was I thinking?" as down, down, down we rush and the momentum of the car pulled by gravity takes us through the inclines and descents of the rest of the ride. Yet we know if we try to unlock our seats and jump out there will be a huge mess. So we hang on and just go with it. There are horizontal curves that pull us side to side and downward rushes into deep ravines, and sometimes we go through the corkscrew and end up upside down. Sometimes we are holding on for dear life, and feeling like we might fly into the air any second. We watch as the ground rushes up to meet us or speeds away, and the trees and sky and ground blur together as the ride takes us past at breakneck pace. Ultimately, all we can do is trust that the ride operator is going to know when to put the brakes on. Most people who get on the roller coaster of marriage and family get on with a happy expectation and an intellectual picture of what it will be like. None of us has any idea of what life will bring, and what it will do to our souls or to our relationships. The difficult ascents, the plunging declines, the unexpected curves come, and many families crumble under the strain. But for those of us who know God, we know that He is our Operator, and we trust in His care. Trust means we know that we will get safely to our destination. Trust means that He built the roller coaster, and traveled on it Himself to be sure it was safe. So we throw our arms up in the air and shout "Yeeeeaaaaahhhh!" at the joyous terror of the ride. Eventually we arrive in Heaven with wobbly legs and a bit dizzy, with mom and dad counting heads as each family member gets out of the cars. But what a great time, what a rush!

If we think of Christian family life as some ideal, we will always be disappointed. Families are made up of sinful human beings living in a broken world. My husband Greg and I had, in many ways, our eyes wide open when we got in the coaster car. You jump in, full of hope and optimism for the future, yet there are always those crazy curves.

Like most of our generation, we like to do things in our own way, and pound out our salvation with fear and trembling. But we have some things going for us: Greg and I have been deeply in love and happily married for more than three decades. Since we both came to the Lord pretty much in our adult years, we don't usually take faith, or salvation, or love, for granted. Our girls, Erin (of the sombrero) and Rebekah (pink karate helmet and goggles), have three older brothers: Joshua, Patrick, and John-Mark. Two things have always governed our parenting: unconditional love and strict discipline. Over the years we have dealt with all the normal stuff with kids: illness and injury, problems at school, sibling rivalry, financial difficulties, losing baby teeth, sports teams, science fair projects, choir concerts, school musicals, church attendance, youth group, Vacation Bible School, and church camp. We also have the added dynamic of being a blended family (I hate that designation), and have done the split custody, visiting parent, custodial parent, child support, and custody hearings.

My husband Greg works for the USDA (agriculturalist, not attorney), as a conservationist. He was going green long before it became popular. Greg was raised on a beef farm in West Virginia. I, on the other hand, was raised in the suburbs of Philadelphia. I attended a high school with more than four thousand students, and my only goal on graduating was to find a college where no-one from my hometown would be, a daunting challenge. I found such a place in Bethany, West Virginia. For me the assets of Bethany College were its small size and its interdisciplinary emphasis. Because of this I was able to blend my eclectic interests and gifts in mathematics and languages. I trained to be a secondary teacher with a split certification in math and French for grades five through twelve. My split certification and broad grade level qualifications ideally suited me to teach in a small mountain school, which is where I got my first teaching job. I taught seven different classes, and had seven preparations.

When I returned to Philadelphia for my fifth year high school reunion (after the inevitable interrogation about whether or not I was married yet, or if there were any prospects) came the repeated questions about, why I (or anyone) would want to live and work in West Virginia. At the time, I remember being confused about how to answer that question. I had applied to many schools close to my hometown when I graduated, but the first job I was offered was in West Virginia, and I took it. It seemed simple enough at the time. Now it is home. While I love Philadelphia and visit when I can, I always miss the mountains. The pace of life here is slower and more peaceful. Family is supremely important to most folks, and neighbors tend mostly to look out for each other. There is still an aroma of faith in almost everyone, even if they are not church goers. Common sense and integrity are highly valued, so people are not so much blown around by the winds of change in the world. There are some down sides; folks are sometimes resistant even to good change, and it is hard to gain acceptance in the community, but it is worth the investment to experience mountain life from the inside. However, I still have not been able to find a good Italian hoagie or even explain what it is; folks want to put mayonnaise on every sandwich, or worse yet, Miracle Whip.

My husband Greg attended West Virginia University for vocational agriculture and graduated the same year as I did. His original plan was to teach in a vocational technical school, but as a student he had signed on with the Soil Conservation Service as a student trainee and was offered a job right out of college. He requested that he be assigned anywhere but Keyser, West Virginia, and in true government fashion, that is exactly where he was placed. Obviously, it was providential, and shows that God has a great sense of humor. My husband Greg and I met in Keyser at a community theater meeting, where he had come with a date. A mutual friend had been trying to set us up, but I resisted. After a few disastrous blind dates I had become wary of the comment, "Hey, there is this wonderful guy you need to meet. He's just a prince." How many times had I heard it? Way too many frogs out there, and kissing them does not transform them into princes. When Greg came into the meeting with his date I remember thinking, "That's great. They make a lovely couple. I hope it all works out;" which just goes to show you how wrong you can be about things.

Long story short, Greg and I attended the same church, he wasn't serious about the other gal, and we started dating — country boy, city girl, a match made in Heaven. Let me just say here, though, that there were some naysayers. Greg was a brand-new Christian when I met him, had just been walking with the Lord for two weeks (he always says that I was his reward from God). Greg had also been divorced, and had a three year old son, Joshua. Some folks who didn't know Greg thought that I was throwing my life away on an immature Christian who had already failed in one marriage. My parents actually liked Greg; a good man with a steady government job; he might get me off that religious kick I'd been on since I was sixteen. This wasn't likely; one of the things that drew me to Greg was his beautiful Christian faith.

I love the energy and passion of new believers. Greg had that joy, that Philippians 3:13 bliss where all the past is obliterated and life starts completely over in Christ. He also wasn't ashamed of the Gospel. I pray before every meal, and shortly after we started dating we met for breakfast and not wanting to embarrass him in public I bowed my head to pray. He said, "Aren't we doing this together?" So we prayed out loud in McDonald's. After the meal, as if in confirmation of our commitment to publicly witness to our Lord, a lady came over with her husband and said how blessed she was to see two young people give thanks together before they ate. If ever there was anyone who was "all in" for Christ, it is Greg. Greg's integrity also impressed me from the first; my husband is a man of honor. His word is his bond, and he is dependable. If doing the right thing is difficult or even inconvenient, he still does it. I was also drawn to Greg's gentlemanly manners — he was so considerate and polite. He opens every door for me, helps me into my coats, walks on the outside near traffic when we are together, and still holds my hand.

Another thing I saw in Greg very early was the tender love he had for his son. As I listened to his story of young marriage, fatherhood, and then divorce, I heard over and over the refrain of deep and abiding love for his child. This three-year old boy was tethered to the heart strings of his father, and no amount of time, distance, or difficulty could mitigate it. I knew what kind of father Greg was from the first moment he spoke of Josh.

"When it's right, you know it!" So said one of my mentors at the Bible conference where I spent my college summers. "You have to know as sure as you know you are saved that you're marrying the right person." Until I met Greg, I hoped that was true, that I would be absolutely positive. But soon after I met him I knew, as sure as I know I am saved, that Greg is my soul mate. Greg has such insight into what's important. As we talked it was clear we agreed on faith, family life, parenting principles, careers and community service, and on how to have fun. So after about three months, we were engaged (and we have taken some flack about the speed of our engagement from our now marriageable aged children).

We were out to dinner one night shortly after we were engaged, and all of a sudden he pulled out a list and started asking me questions. "Where would you go on your dream vacation?" That's easy — I said anywhere with a beach. Then he said, "What are your career goals?" When I asked him why he wanted to know he replied, "Because if you want to be a nuclear physicist, we'll have to start planning now." Nuclear physics is still on my bucket list, but how incredibly wonderful to have a husband who cares about my life's ambitions! Greg is my very best friend. I can always go to him with my joys and my problems, and he is always there for me, he always has my back, and I have his. No doubts, no questions, God put him there in Keyser for me, and put me there for him.

Once we got engaged, we started planning our wedding. My pastor was very concerned, and put us through some very serious pre-marital counseling sessions, including one session that was four hours long for Greg alone that started with the question: "Where were your parents born?" Finally, when he had put us both thoroughly through the grinder he asked me, point blank, "Why do you think you should marry Greg?"

I answered, "Because I believe God is calling me into this marriage, and not to marry Greg would be disobedient."

Then my pastor said, "I can't say anything else." (So that's how you silence a pastor!).

Anyway, on a hot, very hot August day, Greg and I were married in my home church, where the air conditioning broke. It was ninety-eight degrees, the hottest temperature in recorded history for that date, and we sweltered in our wedding finery; I in my long-sleeved wedding gown with a cathedral length train, the clergy in their robes, and Greg in his cutaway tails and afternoon ascot. But to all the skeptics out there, I think we have done alright. We have had years of love, gotten through good times and tough times, and always had lots of fun and laughter. One of the best things Greg has taught me is how to laugh at myself and not take life so seriously. As iron sharpens iron we are good for each other. Just the other day he looked at me and said, "Don't forget, we're in this together." We don't always get things right, I am not saying we are perfect, but we have a good chemistry. God put it all together, and God is also in the details.

Early on, Greg and I prayerfully asked God to make us a whole family. We believed that God, that Master Artisan, was calling us together, like the seemingly unconnected and unrelated pieces of fabric that are sewn together to make a quilt. You can't see the beauty of it or the design until the artist has pieced it together. A marriage is like that always, and when you add a child or children into the mix, life gets exciting. Ready-made family served up fresh and ready to go! We started our married life with a set rhythm, one we chose and maintained for several years — a rhythm that fully included Josh. Greg's custody agreement brought Josh to our home two weekends a month and all summer long. So we made the trips and planned special times for our family of three, weaving Josh into our home, our extended family, and our church. We were trusting God to create a new wholeness for our family. This was taking on a high and challenging call from God, but I believe that when God is the quilter, there will always be something beautiful.

But what about the past? So often, when a marriage has failed, or a person falls seriously ill, or a child born out of wedlock is included in a new family, or a couple adopts a child, you hear well-meaning people say, "Well, this is God's *Plan B* for you." It is as if because of our circumstances, or even because of our deliberate sins, that we are disowned by God, that we are demoted to second-class Christians, or kicked out of the family altogether. I don't believe that. I believe that when things go wrong, and life gets temporarily derailed, there is always a new Plan A. Our God is the God of redemption; He is the God of resurrection, of bringing life out of death. Our God is the One Who, when we sinned and messed up Eden, already had a new Plan A for us waiting in the wings. And that plan did not just repair Eden; God's plan through Jesus Christ re-makes our relationship with God. Originally, Adam and Eve were immortal, and got to walk with God in the cool of the evening. Yet they were bound to this earth and to their human bodies. But we, on the other hand, are bound to our human bodies only as long as the breath of life is in them. While we live on this earth, we can, in the quiet word of one prayer, have God's Holy Spirit come live in our hearts. We get to commune with the Living God every day. We may face trouble and sorrow in this earthly life, but we know that this is not what we were created for. God created us in His image to fellowship with Him forever, because He loves us so much. So when we die, our mortal bodies will fall away, we will slough them off like a crusty old shell, and then we get new bodies, and we will get to live forever with God in paradise. Death is not an end for us, it is only a passage to eternal joy. And God did not simply save our first mother and father, He made a plan to save all of us, to reconcile to Himself the whole world and the creation as well. Talk about your Plan A!

God's great Plan A came through the Lord Jesus Christ, and guess what? He grew up in a step-family, a blended family, the Holy Family.

One of the people in the Bible that has most encouraged me is Joseph, the man God chose to be the step-father of Jesus. Here is Joseph, his affianced bride is pregnant out of wedlock, and Joseph knows it is not *his* child. Yet at God's patient urging and direction, Joseph marries Mary, he gives her the protection of his name, provides a home for her and for Jesus, and commits to being the earthly father of the Son of God. In worldly terms, could any family start out with more problems and obstacles to overcome? Yet here again God is taking troubling circumstances and upheaval and creating a new Plan A. Joseph — who probably had no other ambition than settling down and having a quiet family life with his wife Mary in Nazareth — had to readjust his plans to fit God's great plan. So with courage, commitment, and compassion he takes on this ready-made family. He has to take Mary to Bethlehem, right when the baby is due. Then he has to take her and the baby to Egypt. Then back to Nazareth to live their lives. His life, his career, his location are all dictated by the calling of God on his life, to protect and raise Jesus as his own. Our God is the One Who calls families into being, just as He called Joseph and Mary together as the perfect family for His Son. The beauty of Joseph's life testimony is that God took the troubling circumstances of his life and re-created something beautiful and powerful. God poured out grace to re-make, restore, and redeem a heartbreaking situation, and Joseph walked obediently, with eyes wide open, into his calling to be Mary's husband Jesus' earthly father. Joseph could not change his circumstances, he could not change the past, but he could move forward in faith. And here is the beautiful truth: God always meets us where we are; no matter our past, our circumstances, or our misery, God reaches down to that spot, and begins to design a new Plan A. God may lead us to something completely new and different, or He may miraculously re-make the life we have so that it unrecognizable, but there is always a way of redemption, a way to move forward in faith. For us, our marriage calling was our new Plan A, wholly redeemed, wholly family.

Greg and I planned our wedding for that hot August afternoon just so that Josh could be part of the ceremony. We wanted him to know that he was an important person in the new family, and that we included him in our joy. He was our ring-bearer, and looked so cute in his navy shorts and bow tie, with his blond curls and bright cornflower-blue eyes. We had a small family wedding, Greg's brother was the best man, my sister was the maid of honor, my two brothers as groomsmen, and as bridesmaids Greg's sister-in-law and one good girlfriend of mine to round out the wedding party. It was a wonderful worship service, and we had a reception with a Christian band and everything. All the trappings of a nice Christian wedding, and if there were any naysayers left in the crowd, it was too late to protest; we got past that question about objections nice and smoothly at the wedding, and now it was time for the fun to begin.

Being in a blended family is, in many ways, just like being in a family with two original partners and no step-children. The same principles and rules apply. There is a special dynamic of assimilating marriage and parenting simultaneously, but if you understand those basic Biblical principles, then the work is much easier (you may have missed or skipped over that last bit, but I did mention the "w" word; marriage and family and parenting take work, hard work, and lots of it.). Whether you begin with no kids, or one child, or more, young children or teens, the work is always a factor. To make a whole family takes passion, time, and commitment, and lots of prayer. If the children are traveling between two residences, that adds a whole different dimension, because there are two homes, two sets of parents, and two sets of rules for them. Because I met Josh when he was so young (and I didn't meet him until Greg and I were engaged), I was able to build a relationship with him from a time when he was still at the age of wonder. Still, simply put, being a step-parent is having all the responsibilities and none of the rights, and the only way it works is if the parent and step-parent agree to put their marriage first. Greg honored and blessed me by making our marriage a priority over our parenting, of Josh and our other children. We shared responsibility, we shared authority and discipline, and we shared our love. Greg told Josh that he had specially chosen me to be his step-mommy, and Josh would tell people, usually a random announcement to strangers, "Daddy looked a long time to find my step-mommy; he couldn't pick just anybody, he had to find a special lady to be my step-mommy." Because Greg set the tone early, he paved the way for a good relationship between his son and me. Consequently, Josh derived a lot of security from our commitment. Kids need stability and security, the comfort of routine, especially when they travel between homes. We always made sure Josh had his own room, his own clothes and belongings waiting for him whenever he came, and special times together.

It usually takes time to build up a relationship with kids. As a step-parent, you can't rush in. I did all the mom things, I read stories and played games, made birthday cakes and hosted parties, and pretty soon we had a good thing going. Josh put his order for siblings in early. "Mommy," he said, "I want a little brother."

"Would a sister do?" I asked.

"Yup, long as it's not a girl." I had my work cut out for me.

My father-in-law told me I wasn't going to have any girls anyway. "Honey," he said in that wonderful southern Appalachian twang of his, "I got two sons, and two grandsons, you aren't gonna have any girls." Obviously he doesn't have the gift of prophecy.

CHAPTER 2

Pitter Pattering of Many More Little Feet

A couple of years after we were married Josh got his fondest wish, and a baby brother was born, Patrick. I prayed and prayed that Patrick would be born when Josh could be there, and God was so gracious — Patrick was born on our second weekend with Josh that month, just three days late, and Josh got to come see his new baby brother in the hospital. Patrick was born in five and half hours flat, with dark curls and what eventually turned out to be green eyes. He has darker skin, from my side of the family, because Greg and Josh are both very fair. Josh was overjoyed, and even though by then we had a big enough house to let them each have their own bedrooms, Josh insisted that Patrick share his room. They were pretty great together, and we had a lot of fun with our two boys. I remember a very insensitive friend trying to point out to Josh that Patrick was only his half-brother. Greg looked at Josh and said, "Do you love him the whole way?"

Josh said, "Yeah, Dad, I love him the whole way."

"Then he's your whole brother."

As Patrick grew we realized we had a talker on our hands, beginning early and always thinking out loud. When I read stories to him, he had total recall. If I changed even one word the next time I read it, Patrick would correct me. He loved to socialize, and could charm people with a mere elevation of his very expressive eyebrows. His dark eyelashes were about an inch long, and I remember one envious mother of a daughter telling me it was just unfair for a boy to have lashes that long. Children's sermons were always an adventure, and I trembled when Patrick went up to join the other children for the pastor's lesson. Patrick's comments were always good for a laugh, but often at our expense. Greg and I knew something was coming out of his very fruitful brain when he began a comment with "Well, Mom," or "Well, Dad," not to say we dreaded those occasions, but . . .

One year in our poverty stricken state we found ourselves buying necessities for Christmas presents, and I bought Greg a pair of his very favorite tennis shoes. He was at seminary at the time and had come home one evening from a stress-relieving basketball game with other students. "Honey," he said, "these shoes are shot. I'm afraid we're going to have to bite the bullet and get me some new tenners."

"Well, Dad," says Patrick, "Mom already bought you new shoes and has them wrapped in the closet for Christmas."

Greg looked over at me and said, "You were going to let me suffer for the next three weeks, weren't you?"

"Yup, sure was," I replied. Christmas after all is Christmas, and you can't ruin the surprises for mere health reasons. From that, we learned not to share Christmas or birthday surprises with Patrick in advance of the event. When Patrick was in school he was tested for the gifted program, and his vocabulary and verbal skills were college level when he was still in elementary school. Naturally he excelled in his languages, science and history, and with some personal effort made it all the way through calculus in high school. Some things he has had to work for, but his charm always seems to grease the wheels for his success.

Two years after Patrick, we had another son, John-Mark. Like Josh, he also had blond hair and blue eyes, and was a very large nine pound eleven ounce blessing. John-Mark walked early and got into everything, and was our great cuddler. Athletic as well as affectionate, he had a universal kind of intelligence. Everything he does he does with drive and passion. He played so hard in the daytime he would collapse into a comatose sleep at night. The year he went to kindergarten our county switched to all-day-every-day kindergarten. He went at it with all his heart. When he came home from school I would go to meet him when I heard the door open and sometimes found him asleep across the threshold with his legs hanging outside. It was as if he got home and that was the signal to shut down.

John-Mark is an introvert (very different from Patrick) and also a deep thinker. He only talks when he has something to say, and he absorbs everything before he makes a judgment. If he assesses a situation and feels that there is no benefit to speaking, or no goal to be achieved, he does not weigh in. The year he was six, a little in advance of Christmas, I came into the living room and saw him with his characteristic processing look. He said, very nonchalantly, "Mom, I don't think I believe all this Christian stuff. I think I'm an atheist." Six years old. I couldn't believe it. I was panicking on the inside. Where had we failed? Six years old, and rejecting the basics of the Christian faith. I didn't even know he knew the word "atheist"!

Exhaling slowly to restore atmosphere to the room, I searched about for some response. Then it came — an inspiration of the Holy Spirit! "Well, John-Mark, okay, if that's how you feel," I said, "I guess we'll just have to take all your Christmas presents back."

"What?!?" he squeaked.

"Well, if you're an atheist, you surely don't want to be such a hypocrite as to celebrate Christmas, the birth of Jesus."

His eyes got big and he responded quickly, "That's okay, Mom, I believe in Jesus, I'm a Christian." (For the record, and if you ever have the privilege of meeting John-Mark, he is a most beautiful and profound Christian, and pursues his faith with the same energy and passion as he does everything else).

Soon after John-Mark was born Greg sensed God was calling him to go to seminary. He wanted to pursue a theological education and look into full time vocational ministry. He wasn't sure if he was interested in the pastorate or missions, or something entirely different, but he felt a need to get more education. We prayed about it, we looked at all the ramifications, we made our lists of pros and cons, and decided to go for it. Greg quit his nice government job (my parents were devastated), and we packed up our lives and went off to Massachusetts. It was there that we learned to live on faith and the many different ways one can prepare hot dogs, chicken and hamburger. I still have an ambition to write a cookbook with all the creative ideas I gleaned from those lean years. Not so lean, however, that my biological clock — which thought that in spite of medical science needed to bless me with a pregnancy every two years — failed to function. I conceived yet again, even though Greg was working nights, going to classes, and I was working days and nursing John-Mark, here we were with another child on the way. (You're probably wondering when we found the time, as do I; ships passing in the night, and so forth.).

The months went by as we waited for our new addition. I do exercises and try to walk every day, and one evening as I walked around the seminary grounds a young, obviously bachelor student stopped his car right next to me. I was about eight and a half months pregnant, and "great with child" might have been an understatement because he said, "Wow, lady, what are you having, an elephant? You're huge!" There's one young pastor that would have to work on his people skills — especially with young mothers. Anyway, we had been told by our midwives (couldn't afford a doctor in Massachusetts at those prices) that we were having another boy. The heart beat was slow, about 120 beats per minute. I was relieved. I got out all the boy clothes from Patrick and John-Mark, and prepared for our new addition, Timothy Steven.

It was June, and Greg took Patrick and headed to West Virginia to pick Josh up for the summer. My parents came to stay with me just in case the baby decided to arrive when Greg was away, and of course, that's what happened. Greg and the boys had stopped about halfway through Pennsylvania for the night, and were staying with friends. I called Greg at three a.m. to tell him I was on the way to the hospital. He loaded the boys into the car and as he put it, "left no speed limit unbroken between Harrisburg and Boston." He missed the birth, however, by a couple of hours, which I thought was a shame because I didn't even get to squeeze his hand hard with each long contraction, and let him share in this experience. My labor was longer than usual, and after two and a half hours of pushing, we had a baby! Then we found out why it was so long: ten pounds six ounces, and our baby was not a boy, she was a girl! She popped out, and she was beautiful.

So fat that the little knit caps they put on newborns wouldn't fit her, but she was my girl. We named her Erin Elizabeth (even though we knew she was a boy, we had a girl's name ready just in case). My father and our well meaning friends at the seminary posted signs out all over the apartment building, and that is how Greg found out he had a daughter (no cell phones then). My mom, who had stayed with me in the delivery room (and by the by, those delivery rooms in Massachusetts were gorgeous and even had a Jacuzzi in the bathroom), was tickled to death to have a granddaughter, and *ran* across the parking lot to meet Greg and tell him. I reserved the right of telling my father-in-law, and made that call as soon as I could get to a phone. When I told him how much she weighed, and that she was twenty-two and a half inches long, he said, "Oh, she's going to be a ball player." (To be fair to Pops, Greg has always maintained that his telling me there would be no girls was like throwing down a gauntlet, and that once he said that I was determined to prove him wrong. Of course that is ridiculous and only believable to those who truly know me).

Nine days after she was born I came home to see Greg watching TV with the remote in hand and our newborn daughter on his lap saying, "Look Erin, this is football. This is good." He switched channels, and then, "Oh, look. This is basketball. This is good." Then again, "This is a western, this is good." It didn't take. If Josh is Greg's clone, Erin is mine, all girl. She has Greg's light skin (we call it porcelain on her) and some beautiful curl to her hair (mine is as straight as a poker), but her hair is dark brown and her eyes are grey-blue, and she looks a lot like her mother.

My girlfriends, realizing that I had no girl clothes (and no money to buy them) threw me a wonderful baby shower. I came home with so many little dresses and shoes and hats and all of them were pink and lavender. Greg asked if I was ever going to dress her in anything but pink and lavender. I just smiled and said, "You've got your boys, this is my girl." She still looks great in pink and lavender.

I want to pause here to reflect on my college education. I had a professor who maintained that boys and girls were essentially the same, and that all the differences between the sexes are artificial and are imposed by society. If I could meet that professor today I would tell him that his theory is all wrong. My boys, when they were little, would make a basketball hoop out of anything, a trash can, or a laundry basket. Before they could toddle, they would go over to said receptacle, throw something into it, and then put their arms up in the referee symbol for three points (or a touchdown, they're interchangeable). My first daughter never did that. She would sit by the laundry basket while I was folding, pull out an item carefully selected, and it was usually her father's undershorts. These she would wrap around her head like a kerchief, and then she would preen and turn her head in every direction, as if she were on *America's Next Top Model*. Since I am not a woman who fusses much, I know she didn't get it from me. It has to be inherent, and if I ever see that professor again I will tell him that boys and girls are different from the get-go.

Every morning when I would go get Erin out of her crib, she was never crying but had a smile on her face. Her eyes were so big and blue, and my mother said she looked just like me. My grandmother used to say my eyes were china balls, and that is just what Erin's eyes looked like. In fact, she was that little Victorian porcelain doll, with dark lashes, natural French curls, and a perpetual smile. Her daddy loved her from the moment he laid eyes on her, and when she was about three months old, I remember Greg having a wrestling match with the boys on the living room floor. Josh was twelve, Patrick was four, John-Mark was two, and Greg tossed the three boys about, and they flew through the air like acrobats. Erin was under her father, close guarded between his knees and elbows, while he handled the boys. No baby could have been safer.

Erin was also the first girl on both sides of the family. My parents had only my children at that point as grandkids, but on Greg's side his grandparents were still living and his folks only had grandsons and great-grandsons. Needless to say, she was spoiled with little outfits and shoes, jewelry and bonnets, and lots of fuss. At four months we had her baptized, and my mom brought the shoes I had worn for my baptism, but they were hopelessly too small for her feet (Erin has asked me to state for the record that I was baptized at two months, and was undersized – seven pounds four ounces – because my mom was a smoker; she was baptized at four months and her feet were not unusually large for her age). So my mom bought her a christening gown of white eyelet lace, and of course we took her to have her picture made. The patient photographer worked with her for quite a while, but we could not get her to smile. Shot after shot we took and she was not happy, and that was out of character for her. When it was over, I took off the matching bonnet, and bingo! Erin grinned. She just didn't like that bonnet; hats were just not good in Erin's world back in those days. Then we took lots of nice portraits without the bonnet. That, by the way, has changed, and she looks great in hats.

As Erin grew I noticed she had an uncanny ability with numbers, and her little mind was just as analytical as mine was. She drew logical relationships and conclusions from data she collected naturally and constantly. She was also sensitive and loving, and always trying to make other people feel better. She would fix imaginary meals in her little play kitchen, and bring them around to family. Her sweet spirit permeated our home with a brand new flavor, and I was so happy to have another female in the clan. We thought, of course, that now that we had our girl our family was complete. Which just goes to show you how wrong you can be.

CHAPTER 3

Almost Heaven

The reality of four children and make-piece income took its toll, and Greg and I decided God was calling us back home to West Virginia. God confirmed this when Greg got a new job with the USDA as a district conservationist, and he was assigned to Moundsville, in the Northern Panhandle. He transferred to a seminary in Pittsburgh, and began to work full time, go to classes at night, and pastor a small church across the river in Ohio. How he managed it I'll never know; hours at work, hours in the car, hours in class, and hours in study, and he graduated very well. Greg is one of the hardest working men I know, and one of the most ambitious. He is able to make goals, and then plans to achieve them, and everything he does he does with excellence. He is also one of the humblest men I know. If you met him, you would never suspect that he is a very important man with very important responsibilities. That is because he is also the best listener I have ever met (a gift that I do not naturally have). Within a few minutes he would draw you in to his conversation, and would show such interest and concern in you that you would enjoy sharing your life with him. I have seen him do more ministry on a basketball court than many pastors do from a pulpit, though he's quite good in the pulpit too. I have often said that pastors' wives may change churches, but they always have to listen to the same preacher. For me that has always been a blessing. Greg's messages are always interesting, creative, spiritually challenging, and most often highly entertaining.

Moundsville proved to be a great place for us as a family. We had a good home church, and our kids went to good schools. Our family grew and grew, and yes, I got pregnant yet again. After the initial shock, we got used to the idea of having five children. Rebekah was born two years after Erin, and she was only nine pounds eight ounces (because I very carefully explained to my doctor that having a ten pound baby was no picnic and that letting me go too far beyond my due date could be hazardous to our health — his included). So after an inducement, our little girl was born. Rebekah has very curly dark brown hair, and her father's green eyes. She has the darker complexion, like Patrick, a ready smile, and is the quintessential baby of the family. Rebekah is a social butterfly. She makes friends easily and others find her a ready and friend, and genuine and loyal as well. When she was little, the thing that characterized her was a wonderful laugh. Rebekah, even as a baby, laughed out loud. I took her with me to camp to a women's retreat when she was about eight months old, and we had a ceremonial tea at the outdoor chapel. When they passed the plate of vanilla wafers, she grabbed one in each hand and said, "Cookies," in so deep a voice we all thought Cookie Monster had slipped in amongst us. Then she laughed a deep guttural laugh. As Rebekah grew we noticed in her the same athletic abilities as John-Mark, but she also had music. Rebekah has a beautiful voice, incredible rhythm, and grace in voice and body. She loved school mostly for the social aspects, but has always been a successful student. Science is one of her fortes, which makes her father very happy, and like him, she has an ability to intuitively absorb concepts.

Of course Rebekah was the last to go to school, and she resented very much having to stay with me at home while her siblings went down to the bus stop at the end of our lane. To complicate things, she has a late birthday and the cutoff date made her wait an extra year. "Mom," she would say, "I want to go to school."

"You can go when you're five." Moms have to be so careful about what they say to their kids.

On the fine September morning when Rebekah turned five she got up early, put on her favorite dress and shoes, took her backpack from her room, and walked down to the bus stop with her siblings. A few minutes later, the bus driver herself, who had turned off her bus, arrived at our doorstep asking if Rebekah was supposed to be going on the bus with the rest of our children. Of course I said no, not yet, and Rebekah burst into tears. "You told me I could go when I was five," she wailed. I spent a lot of time trying to explain about late birthdays and school starting dates and all the things that did not make any sense to her five year old mind. I was the terrible villain who had misrepresented the bitter realities of life. So I wrote her a book, a special book, all about how when she went to school the next year, she would be way ahead of all the other kids who have early birthdays. It worked out great, too, because Rebekah met one of her best and lifelong friends the next year when she finally matriculated at kindergarten.

With Rebekah's advent we were full up, and in case you've lost count, we have five kids: two blonds, three brunettes, three with blue eyes, two with green, three boys, two girls, and at the time of Rebekah's birth, Josh was 14, Patrick almost 7, John-Mark, 4, and Erin, 2. Seven, a very Biblical number of completeness, seemed just perfect. Just enough room on the mantel piece for seven stockings, just enough crazy to keep us from getting bored.

I need to add here that Josh came into our full custody just before Beka's birth. For years our family life had been punctuated with the rhythm of Josh's visitation schedule. Time after time, we would travel to get him for the weekends, holidays, or for our summer visitation. Our kids were all part of this, which was hard on them, and especially John-Mark and Erin who inherited their penchant for car sickness from me. And for years our Christmas was December twenty-sixth because our visitation schedule never included Christmas Eve or Christmas Day. Our kids never opened presents until Josh came home, and every December twenty-fifth was spent on the road to pick Josh up at exactly five p.m. We didn't rush home and open presents, we just simply woke up the next morning and had our Christmas a day late. It worked very well when the children were younger, but as they got older they had to explain to their friends why they didn't have their Christmas when everyone else did. Josh came into our home just before his freshman year of high school. Our girls do not remember a time when he wasn't a part of the family full time. And as time went on, the memories of that difficult time faded and our life took on a normalcy we had never before enjoyed.

One of the best things about having two daughters is that they can be best friends. I used to joke that the reason God gave us Rebekah was so that Erin and Rebekah could both have someone to be maid of honor at their weddings. As the girls grew up they played together all the time. We bought them bunk beds, but every morning when I came in to wake them they were either together in the top bunk, or together in the bottom. Going shopping with them is like joining a mutual admiration society. They sing together, do dance routines and drama together. Just to see them laughing and joking is infectious. Of course they fight sometimes, but as far as sisters go, they are amazingly close, and always have been.

Seminary educations are expensive, and for years money was pretty scarce. That didn't bother us, we learned to make do and manufacture our own fun. We only had one car, but we managed. Most of the time I was a stay at home mom — an intentional choice we made for our children. I cooked and sewed curtains out of old bed sheets and table cloths and made life comfortable. Greg continued to advance through the ranks of the conservation service. When you work for the government, you move a lot, especially at the beginning of your career. The USDA likes their conservationists to get a lot of varied experience with land practices, so we saw most of West Virginia and a good bit of Ohio in the early days. We rented lots of different places and sometimes I felt I was better at relocation than I was at staying put. After a few years in Moundsville we were able to buy our first home, and what a great blessing that was! We were thirty-eight when we could finally afford to do this, and we found, or rather, I found, a great house. It was Father's Day, and I saw a house in the paper that looked like it might be big enough for us. Greg had fallen asleep after church, and I went on my own. It was ten miles out of town, and it was up on the ridges of Marshall County. In West Virginia you are either going uphill or down all the time, and this particular ten miles was curvaceous and brought me up several hundred feet in elevation. It took almost half an hour to do those ten miles, and I almost turned back four times. But when I got there, I knew it was our house. Not at all fancy or pretentious, it was a three bedroom ranch, with a finished basement, family room and fourth bedroom, and an addition with a dining room and a fifth bedroom above. No air conditioning, but because it was up in elevation it was wonderfully cool and breezy. There was a great hill out back for sledding. I called Greg and told him, "I found the house the Lord has for us."

He said, without much enthusiasm, "Really?"

I replied, "It has a study with built in desk and bookshelves."

He said, "Come get me."

For those of you who are not married to a preacher, they have a need for a study with bookshelves. There must be books: testaments and commentaries and dictionaries and lexicons and tomes of theology. Then there must be a place to keep them. Finally, there must be a desk at which to read and study the books. If it is not disrespectful to say so, it is an addiction they acquire at seminary, and of which they are never cured. Some pastors even ask their churches to include a monthly book allowance in their salary packages.

As evidence of God's special blessing on the deal, we closed on our house in two weeks, and it was an amazing place to live and raise children. The kids all still think of Moundsville as home, and of that house as the best place we ever lived.

Over the years a lot happened and a lot changed. The children had soccer and gymnastics and basketball and football and piano lessons and trumpet and flute. We attended church every week, and the kids went to Sunday School, family events, Vacation Bible School, and youth group. Religious services were not optional in our family, and we always sat together as a family. We had some special moments in Christmas programs. One year John-Mark decided he wanted to be

Superman instead of a shepherd, and jumped off the stage throwing off his mild mannered alter-ego with a shout that revealed his true super-human identity. Erin tried to remove baby Jesus from the manger that same year mid-performance, stepping out of character as an angel. Another year Erin and Rebekah had a fist fight when Erin tried to recite her prayer and Rebekah stole her thunder. The pastor took a video of it but I was never able to get a copy.

Christian parents often think that engendering faith in their children is a natural. For those of us who came to Christ independent of our families, we think that our kids will get it and will always cling to it, just because they have the benefit of being raised by Christian parents. But the truth is that every child has to come to Christ on his or her own. Every person has to make that commitment, not as an extension of what they have been taught and seen in their parents, but independently. I prayed for all of my children. From the moment I knew they existed I prayed that always they would know the love of God. I prayed for them to know how we loved them, and that they would see the Kingdom of God lived out in the microcosm of our family life. But I also prayed that God would make Himself real to each of them, that all of them would make the decision to follow Christ and accept salvation through Him. But for our kids, the most significant factor in finding faith was church camp.

Every summer the two mandatory activities for everyone were swimming lessons and church camp. Swimming lessons so our kids would never drown physically, and church camp so they would never drown spiritually. Our church camp had a program for kindergartners and primary campers that required a parent to come along, but the parents came for free. We starting going with Josh when he was wee little, and that was great because we didn't have to forfeit any of the time we had with him for the summer. But no good deed goes unpunished, and Greg and I both were sucked into directing youth camps; Greg directed high school, and I directed junior camp (5th and 6th graders).

Our church camp is what you would call "rustic." We slept in cabins with electric lights, the bathroom was several hundred yards down the path. It was on a man-made lake in Ohio, and we swam in the lake. Folks who have passed through that camp all have a great love of it, and most try to spend time there every year. What made it special was the genuine faith of the people there, the sacrificial servanthood of the staff and volunteers, the ultimate authority of the Bible in the organization and teaching, and the mission of sharing the Gospel with as many kids as possible. Going to camp is like stepping into a faith community from the book of Acts, if just for a week. The whole camp is like an impromptu church, organized around the teaching of the apostles. The small groups and cabin groups are like house churches, having devotions, learning and working together. Everyone comes together for a common meal, and then goes off for their various activities, only to come together at the open air chapel by the lake for vespers every evening. Kids come from all kinds of families, and they get to participate in a Christian community in miniature, and experience God's love in that context. As parents, I think Greg and I did everything we could to catechize our children, to bring them up in the fear and admonition of the Lord. But every one of our kids, without exception, says that the place where Jesus Christ became real to them was at church camp.

Church camp is the great equalizer. When you go to camp, everyone is wearing comfortable clothes since it is camp. It doesn't matter if you are rich or poor, and cell phones don't work out there. Everyone smells like bug spray or sunscreen. Camp has all kinds of good stuff you don't get other places: music, games, Bible lessons, crafts, hiking, boating, fishing, and everyone can find something they are good at or something they enjoy. You get close to people when you live with them for a week, especially when the water main breaks on a day when the temperature rises to one hundred four degrees. And at the campfires, you sing and eat s'mores and talk about things you would never speak of at home. You get to talk things out with people, and the counselors are way cooler than your parents, college kids who really rock their faith. Kids like mine, who were raised in the church, get to see faith played out in the lives of others, and see the validity of the claims of the Gospel in a new way. And somehow, being out in the creation, where the skies are spangled with more stars than you ever knew existed, and the geese rise up over the lake in the sunrise, and if you're lucky the eagle will come out in the evening, you find it easier to talk to God, because the busyness of the world and the noise of life is silenced in the peace of the woods. When you are at camp, all the difficulties and drama of your school and group of friends from back home get put into perspective, and lose their power over you.

One of the best things about high school camp was the t-shirt exchange. The kids would all come to camp with a new shirt from their high schools, and everybody would trade. During the school year, they would show up at each other's games and concerts, wearing shirts from various schools. It was a rainbow of school colors, and it showed up in theaters and concert halls and sports stadiums all over the Upper Ohio Valley. They created quite a stir, when kids from rival schools would come to cheer their camp buddies on, and their classmates would want to know how they knew all these kids from other schools.

One by one, my children took their turns going off to camp. They started when they were five and they still try to go every year. And one by one, each made his or her commitment to Christ, maybe at the outdoor chapel, maybe at the prayer rock, maybe at the campfire, or in the gazebo. And to our great joy and eternal blessing, every one of them from Josh on down, turned around and served as a counselor. Patrick and Rebekah also hired on as staff, John-Mark has now followed in his father's footsteps and taught high school camp, and Erin directed junior camp. Camp's great benefit is that we received more than we ever contributed. Our kids not only learned faith in a dynamic Christian community, but they fellowshipped with people from other church traditions. Our camp would often have a missionary staff person from another country: Russia or Kenya or Latin America. The lasting impact on camp and on our kids has been so much for the good, because as they interacted with people from different Christian backgrounds and different cultures, they saw that the grace of Christ is the same throughout the Church and throughout the world. Whatever our outward skin color or culture or rituals, there was always a common denominator of faith, a marker that was recognizable in any person who belonged to Christ. And instead of being a barrier to Christian community, everyone learned to appreciate the gifts and the diversity without losing the focus on Christ. In a few weeks of intensive fellowship every summer a foundation of grace was built in the hearts of these kids, and a kindred spirit among them that expressed itself across the miles and months of the school year with letters and phone calls and impromptu gatherings, as well as lifelong friendships. This foundation became an anchor — one of the many God provided — to tether us to hope during the difficult times ahead.

CHAPTER 4

Life Goes On

As all our kids came up to school age, life became exciting. By the time Josh was in high school we had kids at every level: elementary, junior high, and high school, and why do all the schools plan parent-teacher conferences on the same night? I needed roller skates with rocket boosters to get to all of them. Greg and I divvied up the teachers and schools, and had debriefings with the community when we got home. Josh played soccer, and it was a new program at the high school where the team was co-ed. We went to every game, and I was the treasurer for the soccer moms. He was a great defensive player, and each year got better and better. Joshua was, of course, the first to graduate high school and go away, and he opted for enlistment in the navy. Rebekah, who was fourteen years younger and who considered Josh as a kind of third parent, took this very personally. She could not understand why "her Joshy" was going away. Greg and I had our reservations about his enlistment; we always assumed he would go to college, but it turned out to be the right choice for him. He had done well in school in most subjects, but could not really see the relationship between his work and his success. In the military this relationship is obvious and persistent. Greg's folks came up in October that year and watched the kids so we could go to Josh's pass in review up at Great Lakes. It was a very moving ceremony, and we were very proud of him. Over the next few years he would be deployed on ships, overseas in Japan and the Philippines, stateside in California and at Bethesda Naval Hospital in Washington, D.C., then finally in Hawaii. He was a medical corpsman, and since the marines do not have their own medical personnel, Josh trained with the marines and was often deployed with them. As a corpsman, Josh told me that his life expectancy in battle was less than fifteen seconds; only the radio operator had a shorter life expectancy, because the enemy would try to knock out communications first and the medic second. It was information I would have been happier never to know. But Josh did very well in the navy and I even got to see him receive a medal from the admiral at Bethesda.

The older they get, the more selective kids have to be in their activities. Patrick opted for football, and was an incredible kicker. He could boot a football as far as the coach wanted, and with incredible accuracy. He actually played quarterback in junior high, but by high school he was on defense. This was probably because of his size. Patrick grew eight inches his sixth grade year, and went from five foot three to five foot eleven. Then he grew another three inches. He always retained his position as punter, though, and that is a heavy burden for a football mother; when everyone else is sighing with disappointment I was on my feet cheering for the punter. Patrick punted forty-seven times his senior year and earned the school records for the longest punt (sixty-three yards) and the highest average distance of punts. The team, however, only won one game. It was a great year for a punter, and the local radio station that broadcast the games awarded him the honorary football on the air.

When Rebekah finally did get to go to kindergarten, after that first agonizing disappointment for which she probably still blames me, I re-entered the teaching force, taking a position at a home for pregnant and parenting teens. As a residential facility, it accepted girls who were school age and pregnant, but who had been removed from their parents' care for some serious reason, usually abuse or neglect. This job was at once heartbreaking and fulfilling; I loved working with the girls, many of whom were far behind in their schooling. I taught in an alternative classroom, and our job was to get the girls back to grade level so they could go back to a regular school. Our classroom was a part of the public school system. I however, was part of the agency staff and not deemed a public school teacher. The job was ideal in that my work schedule mirrored my kids' schedule, and I could be at home when they were. I also finished my work on site every day, and didn't have the usual load of paper grading and extra work that most school teachers have. The many stories of the girls I worked with touched my heart; it is so agonizing to me to know that there are parents out there who do not love or want their children, and some that will abandon or neglect them. Worst of all were the girls who had been abused, molested or beaten or burned; it was a job that made me very thankful for what I came home to every night.

Still, there were transitional issues. Keeping up with all the kids and their activities became very difficult. We hit a few rough bumps. By the time Patrick was a senior, John-Mark was playing varsity soccer, and our evenings in the fall were soccer on Mondays through Thursdays, football on Fridays or Saturdays. In between we were still doing Vacation Bible School and youth group and all the great things that that entails. After seven more years of seminary part-time, working full-time, and being a student pastor, Greg graduated from seminary. It had been a total of nine years in graduate school, and he became what those in the business call a "tent maker" - someone who, like the apostle Paul, has a secular career to support the ministry career (Paul's business was tent making). Greg was hired and installed as pastor at a small family church in Ohio part-time. All the members took us into our hearts, and every Sunday we got up early, and after the traditional Sunday morning shoe hunt, we put everyone into the minivan and set off down the mountain and across the bridge to church. Our kids had numerous surrogate grandparents there, and we were loved and supported. I was elected the head of the women's gathering, and the kids went to Sunday school and church with us every week. We started special programs in the church, and of course, did church camp every year.

Erin was involved with lots of stuff during these years, basketball (two teams), choir and piano lessons, and she had a good group of friends she had come up through school with. She loves to design things and sew, and like John-Mark, is pretty much of an introvert. We did a lot of mother-daughter stuff, and I even made the three of us matching outfits, always wanting to provide fodder should they become stand-up comics in future. Erin has always been tall for her age, but thin. We actually had a party for her the day she made it to one hundred pounds; I think she was fifteen. We feasted on Doritos and ice cream, those great health foods.

Rebekah in the meantime was making friends and influencing people. One evening as I cleaned up supper, a little girl showed up at my door with her sleeping bag. Her mother, whom I knew well, waved as she drove off and the little girl said, "I'm here for Rebekah's sleepover." One by one they came to the door and soon nine little girls had arrived; I felt like Bilbo Baggins in an unexpected party. One of the mothers, who was very insightful looked at my resigned face and said, "You had no idea Rebekah had invited all these people, did you?"

"None at all." We brought the TV up to the living room and set up the VHS, and I looked through the pantry for some snacks. It all worked out well, but Rebekah and I had a serious talk about asking permission before inviting the whole female contingent of her third grade class.

I have often felt that I have neglected the musical education of my children, but they seem to have taken care of it themselves. Patrick signed up for piano lessons in high school, and sang in the choir. He learned to play the guitar. At his senior concert, he and a classmate sang a duet of "I Can Only Imagine," and brought the house down. Standing ovation. The next day a little pierced freshman dressed all in black with a Goth look about her thanked him for the great song. At his graduation, seven years after Joshua's, he was handed a microphone and sang a solo. He hadn't even told me, and of course I dissolved into tears.

John-Mark also picked up guitar and then drums. He plays in a praise and worship band in Morgantown. Greg and I were walking around the neighborhood together one night and Greg said, "You know, this would still be a nice quiet neighborhood if some idiots hadn't bought their kid a drum set." It still sits in the garage and gets use when he is home from school.

I thought we would stay in our small mountain community for years to come, at least until the kids finished school, but once again, we see how wrong we can be. A job came open in Parkersburg, and Greg applied, but they offered him another job instead. He came home and asked, "What about Beckley?" Beckley, I thought, where's Beckley?

CHAPTER 5

Seventeenth Movement

Once again, after much prayer and consideration, we felt the Lord calling us to pick up and move. Greg accepted the new job, we sold our home and found another, again in record time, and we moved. This, our seventeenth move, brought us to south-central West Virginia. To say it was an upheaval was an understatement. It was the summer, John-Mark was heading into his senior year of high school, Erin into her sophomore year, and Rebekah was a rising seventh grader. Patrick was at *the* University (for those of you unfamiliar with West Virginia, that means West Virginia University to a large portion of the state, except in the more south-westerly regions where *the* University means Marshall University). We had found a house, down from five bedrooms to four, and Patrick likes to say that when we sent him to college we moved and didn't even buy a house big enough for him to have a bedroom. Josh was a navy veteran by this time, married with children, and he eventually found a job and a home within one and a half hours of ours. We were also close to Greg's parents, so it seemed sort of ideal.

West Virginia is a state with lots of diversity in culture and even in accents. Living in the northern panhandle we were among people who were northerners, mid-Atlantic folk with a typical northern accent. But it was different in the southern part of the state. Our first week there, as we were still unpacking stuff, I ordered pizza. The woman on the other end of the phone said, "Well, hey, honey, that's jest great. We'll have that order out to you right away, and it'll be forty-two fourteen, sweethaart." I thought, "I have arrived in the south, the pizza lady called me 'sweethaart!'"

Soon after we arrived, Greg began preaching, filling in for churches without a pastor. I was hired by a middle school (which in my mind was still a junior high) to teach seventh grade math. It was a great school, a shiny new building with beautiful facilities and a great staff. A perfect teaching environment and by my second year I had my own classroom and didn't have to migrate. We found a new home church and the girls and I joined; Greg, as an ordained minister does not belong to a local church. John-Mark reserved his membership back in Ohio, but attended with us or went with his dad every week (word had got round that an unattached preacher was available, and Greg found himself filling pulpits all over). I taught for two years, but then I was approached by two churches and offered a ministry position which I took. We got involved, at school, at church, and wherever opportunity presented itself. In no time at all, we were as busy as we had been before we moved.

When the kids were little, we moved all the time. We would pack our van and a truck with our belongings, throw the kids into their car seats, and get on our way. This time we were much older, had much more stuff, and the kids had to change school districts as well as schools. I thought that transition would be easy, especially since we were transferring from one school to another within the state, but it was not. I did as much research in advance as I could, and we bought a house in the best possible district for our kids. But the new school was on a different schedule, they recorded grades with a completely different system, and their courses were completely different in sequence. The academic strengths of the two schools were also different, and that impacted John-Mark and Erin especially. John-Mark has always wanted to be a doctor, so the smooth transition of his academic record was imperative, and that was a struggle, one that took months to settle. He did make first string on the school's championship soccer team, and the coach, who is our neighbor, said he felt he owed a fruit basket to our former high school for sending them such a high caliber defensive player for their lineup. Soccer also provided a natural entrée into the social world of our new neighborhood. Rebekah found herself in a much bigger school, and a more urban climate than before. From a tiny mountain school with fewer than three hundred students she was jettisoned into a junior high (I refuse to call them middle schools), that had over a thousand. She joined the choir and the basketball team and soon found her niche. It also helped that she was due to go to the next school anyway, so there would have been a change regardless. Erin, however, had the hardest transition. Her academic record was hardest to transfer. She had been in an accelerated math program that positioned her for Calculus as a junior, and she had already taken Algebra I, Geometry, and honors Algebra II. In her old school she was scheduled for Trigonometry and Pre-calculus, and was considered one of the best math students of her class. I remember her geometry teacher telling me she was the only student he had ever seen who had opted to do paragraph proofs for her problems, as opposed to the common chart proofs. When she completed a test early, she would go back and do the proofs both ways. He was astounded at her skill and dedication, and said an "A" seemed hollow and insufficient as a grade. She completed this course the same year she took honors Algebra II, where she also earned straight A's. As a math teacher, I prayed to have students like Erin in my classes; ones who truly understood the value of math, who were well behaved and disciplined, and who were up for any challenge. I was especially delighted when I had a female student who was able to break out of the stereotypical "girls are no good at math" mold and excel with confidence in what is traditionally a male dominated discipline.

At the new high school, there was much more strength academically in English than in math. Erin's counselors and teachers felt she was not qualified to take the advanced math courses, and encouraged her, directly and indirectly, to change to a less challenging course. There were many parent teacher conferences, and we talked it over with Erin, saying we supported her in whatever she chose to do. She decided to persevere with the harder classes. I tutored her occasionally, but she would come to me with a question, get the answer she needed, then finish the work on her own. Oftentimes Erin was the only student to get the class work correct, and the older students came to her for help on the assignments. She finished trigonometry and calculus by the end of her junior year with reasonable success, but it was no longer a source of satisfaction to her. She excelled in other classes, but the joy she felt in her mathematics had been decimated by this bitter experience. Eventually, however, Erin found some good friends, and started taking karate. After two long years we felt that she had come out of a long difficult transition, and her life was stabilizing. Her compassionate heart found her reaching out to friends who needed a helping hand, and one summer she was part of a mission team that took a Vacation Bible School program to Mexico. When she came back from Mexico, she had lost thirteen pounds, but she had had a great experience and was really excited to share it. The camp manager in Ohio wanted her to come and counsel straight off the plane, but she was too exhausted, and needed to recharge. Soon she bounced back to her cheerful self, and the pictures and stories from her mission trip were inspiring. We had wonderful videos and still shots from the sponsoring church in Wellsburg, West Virginia. Erin soon began dating, first a fellow from karate, and then a boy from church, and then another guy from school. We used to joke that when a prom or dance came along she could always wear the same dress, because she just switched out the escort (and unlike most teen girls, wearing a dress a second or third time was not a problem for Erin). She participated in the Bible Club at school and led devotions for them. She was in the choir, and had several special opportunities to sing solos and do drama pieces. At the end of her junior year we thought things were going well. Once again, we were dead wrong.

CHAPTER 6

Tailspin

I can say without a doubt that that day, the morning I found her in her closet, was the worst, the deepest pit I have ever inhabited. If you had asked me a week, or even a day earlier, I would have told you that things were good. Greg had found a church that needed a part-time pastor, so he got back to his tent making. I had just resigned my teaching position to go into full time ministry; I was so excited to be working for Christ. We had faced some upheaval, but life was taking on a familiar rhythm and a workable routine. I truly believed that we were about to enter a time of new growth and increasing blessing. Just the day before, my two little churches had joined together to give me a welcome dinner. It was Sunday, and the ladies of the congregations were doing what they called, "putting on the Ritz." Shining antique china, real sterling silver utensils at our places, linen table cloths and napkins, and a wonderful feast. It was great to anticipate a job that would allow me more time and flexibility to invest in my family, and paid me more than I had ever made in my life. I remember looking down the long table at my beautiful daughters, Erin and Rebekah, and thinking how blessed I was to have such wonderful girls. And I was right. But I didn't know that despair and desperation were broiling in Erin's heart, right beneath the surface, and ready to erupt.

A lot of things could be said to be contributors to the eruption; the change in schools, the loss of important friendships, the loss of fulfillment in academics that had always been a pleasure and an affirmation of special giftedness, feelings of worthlessness and being alone and isolated. There is also that element of teenage drama that is present in most teens, and especially girls. Since Erin is more like me than any of my other children, I can say I understand it. She is, and always has been, a very sensitive person. The up side of this kind of character is that she is so compassionate to others, she can empathize with their feelings. Most often Erin is found working for the underdog, always befriending the friendless, and trying to see the absolute best in everyone. Erin is also a fierce friend, the kind who will back you to the wall if you are in trouble. I have always cherished her loyalty. The down side of this kind of character is that sometimes we get carried away with our emotions. Everything seems to be a huge deal, whether it is good or bad, everything has far-reaching consequences that are dire or wonderful. Years ago a beautiful saint at a Bible conference told me very kindly that she was praying that the Holy Spirit would fellowship with me in my emotions. It was such a gracious way to inform me that I frequently overreacted to things. For years since then that has been my prayer for myself, and also for my daughters, and especially Erin. Seriously, a person could get emotional whiplash around us.

This "drama queen" phenomenon has gotten a lot of attention in the last few years, but like many other problems of youth, these challenges in character are glamorized and promoted in our culture. So instead of calling ourselves and our children to account for our behavior, and to harness our strengths and struggle against our weaknesses, we are encouraged to just let everything rip. On television, magazines, books, newspapers, and even more on the internet in social networking, blogging, and Youtube, we hear about every dark detail of people's lives. Things that people used to be ashamed of are now openly broadcast, and the more sensational the better for profit. This trend to publicize our worst faults has damaged our culture, and explains a lot of evil that is on the rise in our society: road rage, school shootings, promiscuity, addictions of all kinds, discourtesy, profanity, and of course, suicide. How many teenagers have been backed into an emotional corner from which they felt there was no escape? How many of our children have been humiliated by their school fellows, and now that humiliation has the potential to go viral! What makes a person think that a temporary problem, a crisis that will be over and forgotten in the not too distant future, is so desperate that it requires a permanent solution? This distortion of reality has had dire consequences for so many like our daughter, and with so much information and public fascination with suicide, the means to do oneself harm are all too readily available.

At the same time, Erin was also dating a boy who made us uncomfortable. Although he professed to be a Christian, he was loath to spend time with Erin at family events, and seemed to be trying to build a wall that isolated her from her family. He always seemed to me to be pushing her to break our rules, wearing down her standards by attrition. It was this relationship that was the catalyst for that terrible evening. Apparently the boy had leapt playfully at Erin, tackling her. Greg came out the front door to find the two of them lying on the lawn in front of the house, with this guy on top of our daughter, in front of God and everyone. His blatant disregard for our home, for our daughter, and for our rules threw us into a rage. I wasn't there when this happened, but came home right in the middle of Greg's lecture to Erin about why this was inappropriate behavior and how this compromised her publically. When I learned what had happened, I was just as outraged as Greg was.

It was not a quiet conversation. We were yelling, Erin was trying to justify herself and excuse the behavior, and the upshot was that everyone went away angry and with raw feelings. Such verbal outbursts are rare at our house, and I felt terrible about it. Not that we as parents weren't right about being angry, but there was a better way to have dealt with the problem. After the explosion of anger, I was miserable. I went down to Erin's room, where she was sitting on her bed, sullen, angry and unresponsive. I remember hugging her, and saying I was sorry for exploding, sorry for how I said my piece, yet not sorry for saying it. She said she loved me too, thanked me for apologizing, but did not hug or kiss me back.

I don't ever expect love or affection in return from my children. It is my belief that unconditional love means pouring love on them, but not expecting it back. When God loves us, He loves us without expectation of return. His fondest desire is that we will see and understand His love for us in the Creation and in the love expressed through Christ, and that we will respond, because His love to us is a statement, not a question. So often when I hear people tell their children they love them, it is a question. The pitch of their voice rises, sounding just like an interrogative; it is clear they are waiting to hear the child say, "I love you," in return. But one of the most powerful things we can do for our children is to imitate the Godhead in saying "I love you," with a statement, not a question. Listen to what a question sounds like, and listen to what a statement of fact sounds like. Your voice falls in tone and in pitch when you make a final statement of fact. Your love for your children should be a statement of fact. Say it often and say it with meaning. Say it when it's hard to say and say it with determination. And don't follow it with the conjunction "but". Saying "I love you, *but . . .*" also implies conditions. Just say, "I love you. Always. Completely." That's it. Bam. Done.

All through the Bible, God makes statements about His love for us. Indeed, all of Scripture is a love letter from God, the great story of His salvation, the practical demonstration of ultimate love: "Since you are precious and honored in my sight, and I love you." (Isaiah 43:4 NIV); "I have loved you with an everlasting love." (Jeremiah 31:3 NIV); "The LORD your God is with you, he is mighty to save. He will take great delight in you, He will quiet you with his love, he will rejoice over you with singing." (Zephaniah 3:17 NIV). And then in the New Testament: "For God so loved the world, that he gave his one and only Son, that whoever believes in him, shall not perish, but have everlasting life." (John 3:16 NIV); "As the Father has loved me, so I have loved you. Abide in my love. If you keep my commandments, you will abide in my love, just as I have kept my Father's commandments and abide in his love. These things I have spoken to you, that my joy may be in you, and that your joy may be full.

"This is my commandment, that you love one another as I have loved you. Greater love has no one than this, that someone lays down his life for his friends." (John 15:9-13 ESV).

Over and over again in the Old and New Testaments the love of God is declared to us. But the ultimate declaration of love, the statement of the unconditional love of God is the cross. When Jesus died on the cross, He was thinking of others. His sacrifice, made on our behalf, was made in love. He thought of His disciples, He thought of His mother, He thought of us, He even thought of the soldiers who crucified Him. And He did not expect love in return, because love is only love if it is given away without expectation. It is not a transaction, it is a gift. Our God knew some of us would respond, and so He made the statement of love. In the economy of Heaven, there is no balance sheet of credits and debits, there is only one great gift of eternal love, demonstrated on Calvary, eternally credited to us as the righteousness of God.

One of our toughest jobs as parents is to imitate the love of God, to create that atmosphere of unconditional love for our children. When they are babies, it is easy. Loving a cute little baby is a matter of cuddling and speaking love, and filling physical needs. It may be hard to get up in the middle of the night for a feeding, but it is not intellectually taxing. We want to provide that security for them as infants out of which the sense of love grows. As they get older, you add to the physical and verbal love discipline, that fence of boundaries that reinforces security and tells the children that you love them too much to let their own behavior get out of control. When they get to be teenagers, and start to question all that you have tried to do and teach, it is a time of stretching boundaries without endangering them. Little by little we need to offer them more independence, but always with a safe place to fall. One of our kids wrecked both our family cars in less than seventy-two hours. One accident was not his fault, but the other was. What an opportunity to look him in the eyes and tell him how much more important he was than a car! Or even two cars. But then we have those times, times like our own worst day, when our children make choices that devastate us. They may choose to take drugs, or to become sexually active, or to steal, or to actively oppose every ideal we have ever embraced. If they are still young enough to be in our care, we have to engage in a solution. If they have committed a crime, or are endangering themselves or others, then we are responsible for that as long as they are minors and as long as we are legally their guardians. We cannot control their thoughts and beliefs, and nor should we try to; but we have the right to insist on their lawful behavior while they are dependent on us.

A side note here: my kids have no privacy privileges in our house. Since we are legally responsible for their behavior, they are accountable to us for everything they have. I searched pockets when I did laundry, and in addition to the lucrative paycheck that yielded, I also found some very interesting reading material and objects over the years. Our kids have to keep their bedroom doors open, except when they are changing clothes. When they went to camp, I cleaned their rooms, and that was also an interesting avenue of discovery. I read their diaries and I had the combination to their lockers at school. I did not often purposely pry, but the threat of knowing all their secrets provided a grand sufficiency of fear. In our home, friends and significant others visit in public areas of the house (living room, kitchen, dining room, and when we finally were able to have one, a family room). Phone calls are made in the public area of the house, not in bedrooms. Computer time is on a family computer and also in public areas of the house, and all internet access is carefully monitored by us. There are no televisions or computers or game consoles or phones in their bedrooms, and for years we only had one TV. That meant negotiation for TV time and gameage, but it proved a beneficial development of relational skills. We did not limit the kind of music they chose to listen to, but we did censor the message. The overriding rule of the household was that Godly standards of cleanliness were upheld in body, living space, and entertainment. I am not saying my kids are perfect angels, and that there weren't times when they broke the rules. But there was never any doubt about what the rules were. And there was never any doubt that they were loved. How then did this happen to us?

Invariably the first questions you ask yourself when a child attempts suicide is: "Is this my fault? What did I do wrong? Could I have prevented this?" I have since mulled it over and over in my mind, and I know these same questions have tormented my husband. With five children we did our best to treat everyone the same, to give attention to all of them. I know however, that sometimes Erin's needs slipped through the cracks. We missed one of her concerts because there was a basketball game for Rebekah. Later she told me how much it hurt not to have someone there. There were other ways I am sure that we missed the mark, but that does not explain all of Erin's despair. In fact, I am sure all of our kids could list ways that we did not meet their needs, real or perceived. Truth is, you can do everything right, follow all the advice of the best Christian experts about family life and child rearing, and still have heartache. The better questions are, "Why has God allowed this heartache? What is He trying to teach us? What use will He make of it for His Kingdom?" Of course, when in the middle of the heartache, especially when it is fresh, it is hard to remember those questions. And truthfully, I am still trying to answer those questions.

What breeds despair? What makes a child feel worthless, and desperate? What makes someone think that death is a reasonable and good solution to problem or problems? What kind of darkness creeps into a soul and begins to whisper that things are hopeless? How does that take hold, and how does it come to bear fruit in such an evil way? Where does the first insinuating thought penetrate, eating away at love and family and self-worth and our very value in God's eyes? How do we hear the lies making noise over the music of Heaven? I don't think it is easy to pinpoint or describe how it happens; you find yourself in the middle of it and somehow the pit is so deep and so dark you cannot see the light, you cannot breathe free air, you cannot combat the evil whispers. Erin herself has said she is an anti-statistic; if you ask her, she will tell you that her father and I checked on her all the time. She will tell you we made strict rules, which at the time, she resented. Every day we told her we loved her, every day. We invested in her, and we gave her time and attention. We prayed for her. We thought we did all we could to create a secure and loving home, and still the lies were able to overwhelm the truth: that she was loved, valued, and cherished by God and by us.

On that fateful Sunday evening, when all the yelling ceased, what were Erin's feelings? I guess I'll have to let her tell you.

CHAPTER 7

Erin Tells Her Story

This is a sad story, one about anger, lies, deceit, and death. This is my story. I had just finished my junior year of high school. Things seemed great. It was the summer and just like all of the other teenagers in the world I wanted to spend time with friends and blow off anything of importance and everything at home like chores and family time. Everything seemed to be wonderful. Then, less than a month after I turned seventeen, I found out my true strength and the strength of my enemy when I forced myself into solitude.

What was it that brought me to this point? Was my life really so horrific that I was willing to give myself the opportunity to try to commit suicide? The answer does not lie in any one event or day or even year. The answer lies in the relationship, my relationship with God.

From the outside, I was the perfect girl. I had several friends, a popular boyfriend, Christian parents, and a great church. I led prayer meetings every morning at my school; I was important to the youth group at my church. My best friends and I were all too happy to not be popular, but to have fun spending time together not drinking, not partying, and not having sex. I had everything going for me, right? I was living the perfect Christian girl's life, right?

But what I didn't realize was that I was an instrument of torture being used to not only to hurt myself, but others that I loved. If you could have looked closely at me, you might have seen the fights I had with my parents, the destructive relationships I had with my friends and the lack of a relationship with my Savior. Having "everything" didn't make me happy or strong or fill the void growing in my heart. Having "everything" was what I thought I wanted. My mom often says, "Be careful what you want, because often, God gives it to you and then you realize why He was keeping it from you for so long." "Everything" means nothing without Christ.

However, listening to my thoughts you would have heard the lies that I was constantly being fed by others and primarily by my own demons. All day, every day I heard: You are worthless. You are ugly. You will never be good enough. Why aren't you more like the other girls? You are manipulative and mean. No one wants to be around you. Your make up is hideous and fake, just like you. You are unwanted. You are worthless. You are nothing. Who could love you? Why would they love you? You are worthless. And everyone hates you.

I could hear these voices in my mind every day. My dreams were polluted with the stench of my own useless existence. Every cruel thought and action I had ever committed, every stupid, silly mistake was replayed to the song of my life. A song I had written and now, I could no longer drown out the continuous ringing in my ears with the happy and joyful words that I spoke to others trying to convince myself that I was more than a failure. It didn't matter how many times people told me I was beautiful and skinny and sweet, my song told me I was the worst kind of vermin and not worth stepping on.

The one most painful word that I remember hearing and consequently feeling, was WORTHLESS — I know that I have used this word a few times and this is why: if you have ever felt worthless, you can understand my pain. I had been feeling worthless for so long. During the months leading up to my attempt, I remember taking cords and wrapping them around my neck so I could feel the physical pain of the emotional pain that I was not allowed to show to anyone. I was the perfect girl and I had to stay that way because I was already a disappointment and I couldn't let anyone down more than I already had.

The night that I made my attempt was like any night. I had spent the day with my boyfriend (at that time). He had just brought me home and tackled me in the yard when he leaned in for a kiss when my dad walked out and demanded my immediate return to the house. You see, to my dad, the scene he was looking at was much more dangerous to my virtue than I realized. When my mother came home, my dad told her what happened and they began to discuss a plan of action because the next day I was supposed to leave for a retreat with my church. I could hear them arguing in the room next door.

Anger. All I could hear was anger. I didn't know how to make it stop. It drowned out everything, I couldn't hear words, just anger. I didn't know how to take back everything bad that I had ever done. There was too much. And it was too dark. There were things that they didn't even know had happened to me, things that I had done that couldn't be forgiven. These things could never be brought to the light because then I would be exposed. I would have all the shame and sadness and anger that I was so busy putting a happy face over brought into the light and people would know exactly what kind of girl I really was. They would know that I hated who I was. That I had been hurt in the past and that I was vulnerable. They would know that I was not perfect or interesting or good or worth anything. I was so caught up in the anger and I had to make it stop.

I looked around my room and spotted the bottle of medication that I kept for my allergies to help me sleep. I knew that this could help me to stop crying and go to sleep. I opened the bottle and took two pills out. Walking as quietly as possible I went to the kitchen and got a glass from the cabinet and filled it with water from the refrigerator. I went back to my room and swallowed the pills. Nothing happened. What seemed like forever passed by, nothing happened. I looked at the bottle in disappointment.

I could still hear them arguing so I took four more pills out of the bottle and swallowed them. Slowly, pill by pill, lie by lie, I swallowed them all. I knew what I was doing. I knew that things would only go down from here but I had gone too far already. The lies of my past seeped into my head again. The poisonous words worked their way into my heart and I put my earthly remedy to my lips and I swallow. I knew what could happen. I didn't plan on it but I knew that it was possible for me to die this way. I didn't care. I said a prayer for my family, friends, and myself. And I didn't care.

I – Did – Not – Care. I knew what I was doing would hurt them. I didn't care, because that was the point when all the lies that I was telling myself poured in like a waterfall: I am worthless. I am no good at anything. No one really likes you. Boys only want to use you to satisfy their physical needs because that is all you are good for. You could never help anyone you can't even help yourself. You are cruel and selfish and pitiful. You will die alone and unloved. How could anyone love you? You are nothing.

I was abandoned and I didn't care. My truth was so far from THE truth, and I didn't care. I knew it was wrong, and I didn't care.

I took every pill in that bottle. Then, I walked to the kitchen again and grabbed some painkiller and more allergy meds out of the cabinet and finished off both bottles. I couldn't stop. Half way through my binge, my sister came in to talk to me. She just wanted to see if I was alright and I assured her that I was. She left my room unconvinced and I did not care. I continued my attempt to drill out the pain and anger and deceit that plagued me.

At this point I was beyond saving by any mortal hands. My sister, my hero could not have saved me. My parents that I loved and that loved me could not have saved me. Boyfriends, friends, admirers, family, past loves could not save me. I could not save me. My lies and my actions could not save me. So seeing no hope I plummeted into the darkness in my own mind and heart.

I felt a release as I fell asleep that night knowing that it may be the last time I fall asleep here in this world of deception and anguish, but I was not free. I was trapped in myself. I was a prisoner to my own mind that replayed every failure and memory of treachery I had committed. I was simply giving up. I was giving up the idea that I could be saved. I was telling God that He was not enough and that even though I knew He could save me, I wouldn't let Him. I fell asleep that night spitting in the eye of my Lord and my Savior, Jesus Christ, my one true King.

CHAPTER 8

In the Fire, In the Flood

When our children make devastating choices, and the consequences of those choices come crashing down and bring a halt to normal family life, this is when our faith, all that we have believed for all these years, is tested. I found Erin, as I have said, in her closet. She was not unconscious, but she was incoherent. Her speech was slurred, and she couldn't stand up. I shouted at her, shook her, but she just kept babbling. I ran to get my husband, and we got her up to the living room. "What did you take?" he kept asking her, "Erin, what did you take?" She just kept answering us in gibberish. I was standing there dazed and he looked at me and said, "Get dressed, we have to get her to a hospital." That shook me out of my stunned inaction, and I pulled on the first clothes I could find, grabbed my purse. Her daddy picked her up in his strong arms, and put her in the car and we took her to the hospital.

I checked her into the emergency room, and at that hour of the morning they were not busy. We had to make calls, Greg had called work from home, and I called from my cell. Erin had been scheduled that very day to go to a huge youth conference for our denomination (thus the suitcase), and we had to inform them she wouldn't be going. We called the pastor of our home church (Greg was between churches at the time), and then called family and a few people for prayer support. While we waited on the doctor, we had a space of time to breathe, and we both were overcome with grief and remorse. Was this all our fault? I remember looking into the eyes of my husband across the narrow hospital gurney that held our daughter's form as tears rolled down our cheeks. We held each other tight, and the habits, the routines of a lifetime of marriage kicked in. We prayed, we kept telling each other we loved each other, we proclaimed grace and assurance to each other. And we spoke grace to the rigid form of our beloved child, whose sweet personality, whose sweet soul, seemed at a too far distance to reach. We kept telling her we loved her, hoping that familiar voices on the wings of love, love that had been expressed to her every day of her life, would somehow cross the chasm of the drugs that kept her conscious mind imprisoned. We prayed for her. We kept looking into her vacant eyes for a flicker, a spark of recognition. Imploring the Lord of life on the grounds of our eternal relationship with Him, we asked for life for our child. We proclaimed grace to her, and assurance; all the promises of God that all have their "yes" in Jesus Christ.

The emergency room staff came in to interview us. Then came a barrage of questions and we answered as best we could, but we didn't know what she had taken. We called Rebekah, who was still at home, and asked her to go into Erin's room and look in the trash can. I was so torn, I wished I could be at home with my little Rebekah, while I knew I had to be there with Erin. Rebekah was fourteen, and it was a pretty horrible day for her, a growing-up-fast day. All by herself at the house, she went through the trash, and called us back with a list of empty bottles she found in the trash can. They were all over the counter medications, common things you probably have in your own medicine chest. We figured out that Erin's overdose was random, just grabbing what was to hand without a researched plan of drugs that would definitely kill her.

Finally the emergency room doctor came in, and he looked at Erin and asked if she was normal. There are only a few times in my married life that I have seen Greg that angry with a stranger. He towered over the doctor, and he got right in the man's face. "Normal?" he demanded, "Normal? Does this look normal to you?" Then things started to happen. The doctor actually examined Erin, and gave instructions for an I-V and some blood tests and urinalysis.

This was easier said than done. Some OTC's are uppers, some are downers, some are hallucinogens. Erin had taken some of everything. She was restless and wouldn't sit still. She kept trying to get out of the bed and she couldn't clearly understand instructions. One of the nurses and I took her to the bathroom, we got her changed into a hospital gown, but it was like a WWF wrestling match without the costumes. Then they bought her back to her cubicle in the emergency room, and we tried to get her to lie down. At one point when I was struggling with her (and she is a good deal taller than me as well as younger and stronger), she looked at me and said, in a very angry voice, "You can't tell me what to do, you're not my mother."

"As a matter of fact, I am," I responded.

For some reason that got through the fog, and she said, "Oh," and actually stopped fighting me, collapsed and lay back in the bed, settling down for a few minutes.

The hospital staff had to catheterize her, and they did finally get an I-V line run, then they all left and went to their desk in the center of the ER, at which point Erin got out of bed again. I was trying to wrestle her down when she popped her I-V, and blood spurted everywhere from her arm. I had to yell for help, and they came back in, helped get her in back in bed, and fixed the I-V line.

At some point in these proceedings our pastor arrived with his associate. He was unwell that day, so he prayed a brief prayer with us and left. We notified the elders of my churches, and two of them offered meals and help in whatever way that was needed.

Erin was admitted to the hospital, and they put her in a private room in the pediatric section. Josh was working for a doctor at the time of this crisis, and he became our lifeline. Since Erin's regular physician did not have privileges at that hospital, we had unfamiliar doctors working with her, assigned by the hospital. Everything they ordered we reported to Josh, who checked with his doctors and reported back to us. For instance, we wondered why the doctors did not order her stomach pumped, but with the particular cocktail she had mixed, it wasn't appropriate. She needed instead to be hydrated, and getting her to drink was a challenge. Everything became a waiting game.

Soon Patrick and John-Mark arrived from Morgantown. They just dropped everything and came to their sister's bedside. One of my greatest concerns was that Beka was alone at the house, and now we had lots of people. We prayed and talked and cried, and took turns sitting with her. I finally went home to get a much overdue and much needed shower.

As the hot water rushed over me, I just continued to cry and cry. It was the first moment I had had to think, and as I tried to process all the intensity of the last couple of hours a thought came to me, as loud in my head as if someone had spoken aloud: "You're a bad mother." I knew it was of the enemy, but I was so overwhelmed I could not counter it.

I sank down, physically overborne by the grief of that condemnation. Then just as quickly, and even louder I heard God say in my heart, "You are not a bad mother. What you do from here on shows what kind of mother you are." I knew then that God was going to help; I knew there would be a way to be the best mother I could be in the circumstances. I quickly finished my shower and hurried back to the hospital.

Erin was still talking gibberish, still restless, and at times violent. I tried to clean her up, but she fought me so hard that I just had to reconcile myself to her being grubby. At one point she flung out a random punch and hit me square on the jaw; those karate lessons were really paying off. Sometimes when she was hallucinating, she would reach up and start picking at my sweatshirt, as if she were removing imaginary dust bunnies or spiders from my sleeve. All the time she did this she babbled incoherently, and I just let her pull at my clothes and told her I loved her. Sometimes she exhausted herself and lay there, eyes wide, unfocused, and motionless. I laid my hands on her frequently and prayed and prayed and prayed that God would spare her and bring her back to us. The hospital staff brought in a cot so we could stay with her around the clock. Greg never lay down, and if he was not sitting with Erin he was right by her side in a chair next to her bed. He never slept.

Patrick and John-Mark amazed me most. They took turns sitting with her and keeping her in the bed. Sometimes she was intelligible. On one of these occasions John-Mark was with her, and she started to get up. He held her down and told her she needed to stay in bed. She kept fighting him and saying, "I have to get a shower!"

"You don't need a shower, sweetheart," he said, "you smell wonderful, you smell better than I do." She relaxed in his arms and fell back on the bed. The kids came and went, each and all of them taking turns sitting with Erin, or running out to get food, or going back and forth to the house. A pediatrician and a psychiatrist came in to see Erin and talk to us, and the day dragged on as we sat vigil at her bed.

Lots of things were happening during these hours. The hospital staff came in and out, checking on Erin, bringing her food trays that she never touched, and drinks that she needed to keep consuming. They monitored her vitals, and they tested her for kidney failure and other permanent damage to her body. Everyone was so kind and considerate to us. They also gave us as much space as possible, and allowed our family full access all the time. Sometimes it was just me or her dad, other times all of us sat around on the chairs and the cot just watching, waiting, praying, and talking. There was no significant change in her condition. When I wasn't in Erin's room I was either on the phone researching Christian counselors in our area, or picking the brains of the nursing staff for local options.

Finally, in the evening, the psychiatrist came in and said he had a drug to try on Erin. It was an injection, and it might bring her out, but he wasn't sure if the effect would be temporary or if it would end the nightmare. We gave our permission, and the nurse came in with the injection. I happened to be alone with Erin at the moment, everyone else was getting dinner. The nurse came in, brought the injection and her supplies to the bedside. She picked a place out, and carefully gave Erin the shot. My eyes never left my daughter's face as I watched anxiously.

It was like a miracle, an immediate healing like the ones in the Bible. All of a sudden, Erin started to come back to me, like a person coming up from deep water and breaking the surface and gasping for air. Her eyes cleared, her face brightened, and she recognized me for the first time in more than a day. She burst into tears, fell into my arms, and just said, "Mommy, I'm sorry, I'm so sorry." I was crying again, just holding her and thanking God for her deliverance.

It was a short-lived reprieve. Within two hours the drugs still in her system overpowered the injection, and she was hallucinating and babbling again, and we went into a long night of watching and waiting. My husband insisted that I lie down on the cot in the room and try to sleep, but at best I only dosed. I turned so I could see Erin from my pillow, and my eyes were drawn like a magnet to her, unwilling to close in case there was any change. I remember that every time I opened my eyes, someone, most often my husband, was sitting with Erin, holding her hand or just lightly touching her, and everyone else was there quietly keeping vigil. Sometimes I heard gentle conversations, sometimes silence, but round the clock her family was with her. We never left her alone, and Josh called regularly for updates and to get us more information. I don't think he slept that whole night either. We descended together into the valley of the shadow, walking together the path that was marked out for us, knowing for sure only that God was with us as He had promised.

CHAPTER 9

Through the Valley

I keep a quote from Helen Keller in my Bible. It says: "Unless we form the habit of going to the Bible in bright moments as well as in trouble, we cannot fully respond to its consolations because we lack the equilibrium between light and darkness."[1] Her insight amazes me, that a woman who had no living memory of sight or sound had deeper spiritual insight than many of us who see light and darkness with our eyes. Our spiritual treasury of Scripture is what comes rushing to our aid when we are in distress; the promises of God squirreled away are pulled out and cracked open when times are tough. The discipline that our sister Helen speaks of is that of spending time in God's Word daily, and having it as our constant companion. It is not an accessory to life, it is our lifeline. When I think back to those dark hours, the Scriptures that ministered to me most were ones that I had long ago committed to memory. From Lamentations 3:21-26 (RSV): "But this I call to mind, and therefore I have hope: the steadfast love of the LORD never ceases, his mercies never come to an end; they are new every morning; great is thy faithfulness. 'The LORD is my portion,' says my soul, 'therefore I will hope in him.' The LORD is good to those who wait for Him, to the soul that seeks him. It is good that one should wait quietly for the salvation of the LORD." And from Habakkuk 3:17-19 (ESV) "Though the fig tree should not blossom, nor the fruit be on the vines, the produce of the olive fail and the field yield no food, the flock be cut off from the fold, and there be no herd in the stalls, yet I will rejoice in the LORD; I will take joy in the God of my salvation. God, the LORD is my strength; he makes my feet like the deer's he makes me tread on my high places." And from Romans 8:38-39 (KJV) "For I am persuaded that neither death nor life, nor angels nor principalities, nor powers nor things present, nor anything to come, nor height nor depth, nor any other creature shall be able to separate us from the love of God which is in Christ Jesus our Lord." Most of all, these words from Isaiah 43:1b-3a (NIV) "Fear not, for I have redeemed you; I have summoned you by name, you are mine. When you pass through the waters, I will be with you; and when you pass through the rivers, they will not sweep over you. When you walk through the fire you will not be burned; the flames will not set you ablaze. For I am the LORD your God, the Holy One of Israel, your Savior. . ." And from Isaiah 49: 25 (NIV) "I will contend with those who contend with you, and your children I will save."

Funerals often start out with the words: "In life and death we belong to God." There are no guarantees in life; only in God are we given any promises. Many of these promises assure us that we are loved and favored by God as His own, but none of us can escape this world alive. As I sat by Erin's bed that long night, I knew that she might not survive. It was not only the drugs warring within her body, it was the dark despair that had driven her to attempt suicide. There was a battle not just for her life, but for her soul.

When I was a teenager, I had contemplated suicide. High school is not a time I should ever want to revisit; I was unpopular and awkward and lonely and miserable. And I was not a Christian. I was a church goer, I warmed a pew practically every Sunday, but I was full of despair. It was the total feeling of being unworthy and unlovable that brought me to Christ in the middle of my junior year. It was the sudden rush of God's love, that love that accepts us just as we are and makes no demands on us whatsoever, that is what drove me to declare my allegiance to Him as Savior. And it was through a Bible club at school, not through my church, that I came to Christ. After I accepted Christ, I never thought seriously about suicide again. I was still in the same high school, I still had the same problems, but there was a freedom and hope that had never before been part of my life. When Erin acted on her despair, and attempted to take her own life, the most inexplicable part to me was that she was a professing Christian. She had the knowledge, she had the experience of God's love, she had the support system in her family, and yet she took the step that I never dared to; she actually attempted to end her life through overdose.

The darkest path any parent can walk is the loss of a child. I don't care if it is through miscarriage, or through cancer, or through a car accident, or through a lifestyle choice, through drug abuse, suicide, or through natural causes. I don't care if the child is young or old. The very first funeral I ever conducted was for a fifty-eight year old man who died of a heart attack. His mother, in her eighties and confined to a wheelchair, was the person most devastated at the service. She attended her son's visitation, and the worship, and was brought by car to his graveside in the cemetery. For this woman, the pain was of a specialized and acute kind. It is against the natural order of things that any child should precede his parents in death. For a mother and father to look in the face of this particular demon can be shattering to our faith. When servant after servant came to inform Job that his wealth and flocks were destroyed, he stood and heard the news. But when the news of the death of his children came, he tore his robes, shaved his head, and fell to the ground. Then he worshipped saying: "Naked I came from my mother's womb, and naked shall I depart. The LORD gave, and the LORD has taken away; may the name of the LORD be praised." (Job 1:21, NIV). His wife did not deal with everything as well as Job did, in chapter 2 and verse 9 she says, "Are you still holding on to your integrity? Curse God and die!" How we deal with the initial impact of such a devastating loss as the death of child is not to be judged; everyone suffers a disconnect in the first revelation of such pain. To lose not one child, but seven sons and three daughters all in one terrible accident, can any of us blame the bitterness in the heart of Job's wife? Some of us may be able, like Job, to submit immediately to God's sovereignty and worship. Some may lash out at God or others, as Job's wife did. And Job, although he never cursed God, surely questioned Him, as we witness in the next forty chapters. Feeling grief and sorrow and remorse and anger and guilt and all those other emotions is natural in the wake of this immense kind of tragedy.

We ask why, why, why, does something like this happen? I have heard a lot of answers to that question over the years, some better than others. The simple truth is that we live in a broken world, and we are all broken people. Even when Christ saves us, and comes into our hearts and makes His home with us, still He does not remove us from this broken world. We are called to live on in this world, and be in it but not of it. Jesus said, "In the world ye shall have tribulation, but be of good cheer; I have overcome the world." John 16:33 (KJV). God brings things into our lives to teach us. Nothing comes to touch us unless He has first screened it and filtered it. These events are not sent to break us, but to help us grow, to help us trust Him more, to receive the blessing of surrendering to His Lordship. We renew our faith when we hit rock bottom, and have to go back to that blessed place when we first realized we are fully dependent on Him. Every day of our earthly journey we are being changed, transformed more and more into His glorious likeness. And finally, God trusts us with trials. He gives us things to deal with, never more than we can bear, so that we can step out in faith. Remember Job? What was the catalyst of his trial? Satan wanted to prove God wrong. Satan wanted to show God that Job would cave. God, however, trusted Job to stand the test. God said, He even pointed Job out to Satan, He said, "Have you considered my servant Job? There is no one on earth like him; he is blameless and upright, a man who fears God and shuns evil." Job 1:8 (NIV). We are the chosen champions of God this side of the Resurrection. We are the ones that He sends out to do battle. Our enemy does not discriminate; he does not stop at using any torment to break our faith. He is not lazy, nor will he stop at attacking our children. But God promises eternal and powerful resources. All the resources of Heaven are available to us on request. "If God is for us, who can be against us? He who did not spare his own Son, but gave him up for us all — how will he not also, along with him, graciously give us all things?" Romans 8:31,32 (NIV).

The startling truth of these verses, and one that we often overlook, is that God Himself has looked into the face of this demon, the loss of a child, Himself. God understands, so very personally, the bereaved soul that faces the pain of letting go of a child. When our children are hurting, we feel impotent and angry and helpless to aid the little ones whom God has entrusted us to our care. We feel we cannot protect them or relieve them. And no matter how old they get, they are always our children. Our babies. God felt the same way when Jesus went to the cross. God's heart was wrenched with this same deep sorrow. As Jesus hung suspended between heaven and earth, His soul engulfed with the wrath for all of humankind, God the Father knew the depths of every parent's most desperate nightmare. His heart is moved for our grief like no-one else's. Moreover, this is how God loves each of us; He is our Father, we are His children. He loves us more than we can even imagine. He loves our children so deeply, so tenderly, and more than we ever could ourselves. When we come to God's heart with this kind of grief, it is to a heart that fully understands the pain of bereavement, the pain of loss. His is the heart of pure love and compassion. A. W. Tozer writes: "He [God] takes no pleasure in human tears. He came and wept that He might stop up forever the fountain of human tears. He came and bereaved His mother that He might heal all bereavement. He came and lost everything that He might heal the wounds that we have from losing things. And He wants us to take pleasure in Him. Let us put away our doubts and trust Him."[2]

This, then is the God we serve, the God Who loves us from all eternity. This is the God we worship, the God Who gave His all so that we could live with Him in eternity. This is the God we proclaim, the God Who is present with us in the person of His Holy Spirit. Can we, then, trust God with our children, trust God with not only their lives but their souls, and trust Him with the future?

Yes, yes, and again yes.

After a few hours, the doctor wanted to try another injection of the same medicine. I was not enthusiastic, since my first hopes had been raised and then so savagely dashed when Erin submerged back into the abyss of her overdose, but we agreed to try it. Once again we watched, and as before, Erin came up from the deep waters and broke through the surface of the drugs that held her captive. The same thing happened. She breathed, her eyes suddenly focused, and she realized who we were. Again we were weeping and she was apologizing, and we were embracing her and telling her how much we loved her. We knew that this lucid state might last for only a short time, and we wanted to make sure she knew how much we cared about her. The minutes ticked by and she seemed all right. We all sat there and talked, almost like it was a family dinner, but with a wary eye on Erin, to see if this would last. The one hour mark passed, then two, and our hope surged stronger. Then three hours, and more, and the nurses said she was probably out of the woods. We thanked God, we hugged Erin and each other, we cried a little bit more. My husband, who had not slept in almost two days, went home and went to bed. Erin, her body exhausted from the drug induced sleeplessness, finally closed her eyes and slept. I stayed in the room with Erin, but just dosed. I kept checking on her. She didn't awaken, and in the morning (was it Tuesday or Wednesday? I couldn't remember), we had some breakfast together.

That morning the doctors came in and began to interview her, the pediatrician and then the psychiatrist. When a child attempts suicide there are certain protocols, and a limited number of options. Sometimes the professionals recommend committal to a program, sometimes outpatient counseling. We had been warned about certain programs locally, and were hoping that Erin would be able to come home with us. However, we had some leads for Christian residential programs that we could use if necessary. God graciously allowed us to take her home.

Since this was a first attempt, and there was no history of drug abuse or other factors, Erin was prescribed outpatient counseling therapy.

One of our greatest blessings is that Erin sustained no permanent damage to her body from her attempt. The drugs she took could have destroyed the function of any one of several systems, but they did not. This is a miracle, our miracle. She literally had a physical healing that is inexplicable without the protection and direct intervention of God. The healing of her soul would be more gradual and care intensive.

I spent a lot of time with her that morning. The nurse came in and removed the catheter, and Erin finally got to take that shower. She was grateful to get into street clothes again, and then we were able, late in the day, to take her home. It was like walking in a dream, so good to have her alive and safe, and yet feeling like everything was not quite real and solid. Everywhere I looked, I saw the fragility of life and the precarious nature of all that I had formerly thought secure. Seeing their sister safe and sound, the boys had to hurry back to Morgantown. They had left summer classes and jobs to come spend those desperate couple of days with us. We all said good-bye, and began to try to restructure our lives around this new reality. What does Erin remember about that time? What did she learn from her experience? Her own words describe it best.

CHAPTER 10

Erin's Epiphany

I couldn't tell you the exact turning point because I was unaware of the happenings of the next several days. People came to visit and I did some funny things. My family was with me, but my God was hard at work. He was changing me from the inside out, beginning with my heart. I wouldn't realize it until years later when I found that I was not alone in feeling solitary.

When the devil gets a foothold in your life, he tries to claw his way to the surface and cause you to question your reality. This is easier when a person is in a state of confusion and very willing to change themselves to please others, that is why, in my opinion, teen suicide is so high. Satan takes what we desire and distorts it until there is nothing left but the perverted wish of fitting in, or being thin, or needing someone to love you with physical affection. As a young adult now, I can see where my desire to feel love from others was twisted and mutated into an image of hate and anger.

Everyone makes mistakes and everyone has regret. It is natural and something that is difficult to control and overcome. Why do I write this? Well, too often we allow regret and past experiences to dictate our behavior and our future. I know from personal experience that the only future we have is in Jesus Christ and without Him, there is no life. When we are young, we are led to believe that we are not living until we are paying for everything ourselves. You are living now. We are all living at every stage of our lives.

Do you know when those pesky alerts pop up on your computer and they ask you to update something and you always do? So often we treat God like those icons. They are annoying because they take us away from "important" things like e-mail and Facebook. We go to church because our life after death depends on it but really it is just taking away from our "busy" lives. God is so much more than just a one time commitment and a renewal every sixty days. God is a lifetime event starting now and ending never. God is a Father looking after His babies and hoping they do the right thing. God is a subscription that we should be reading every day, allowing the change He makes to happen to us every day. God is constant and being a Christian is too. There is no soft-serve Christian option at the ice cream bar. This is a contract that causes people — even the most unlikely candidates — to change their minds and hearts. It causes love and joy and peace. It causes a unique effect that has no equivalent. It is the best feeling in the world. It is constantly being in the presence of a great Friend, Father, Mentor, Brother, and Messiah. Being a Christian is an action and a lifestyle. It is for the fearful that wish to be without fear because they know that no matter what obstacles lay ahead the Lord of all creation has their back. Christianity is for the people willing to go where God will send them because they know that it is for His glory and not theirs. Christianity is the best decision I ever made.

Because of this experience I don't want anyone to have to feel the way that I did. I hate the taste of the water in my refrigerator at home. It is very difficult for me to take any kind of pill and I can barely stomach watching other people take pills. But these feelings are only the physical effects. My life today looks completely different from life at seventeen. There are so many friends that I would have never met, people that have changed my life and saved it in different ways. Yes, I struggle with the same problems and desires, but I know that God does not give me a problem that I cannot overcome with His help.

I cannot tell you how many times I have thought about suicide since that day. I was not thinking, "Wow, I wish I hadn't done that." I was thinking, "Man, if I had not tried to commit suicide at seventeen I think I would now, and I think I would succeed now." The reason I am telling you this is because I found my strength. I found where my strength came from. I somehow knew that God was keeping me here for a reason and that my time here was not finished. God does not make mistakes.

I said at the beginning of this monologue that this story was about anger, lies, deceit, and death. I was angry. I was lied to by Satan (who uses everyone and everything that he can). I was deceived. And I killed that overwhelming urge to end my life. I will not try to commit suicide again, but I will forever wear my scars.

"For I know the plans I have for you," declares the LORD,
"plans to prosper you and not to harm you,
plans to give you hope and a future."
Jeremiah 29:11 (NIV)

God has a plan for my life and God has a plan for your life. You have the opportunity to change the world and to save a life you didn't even know was in jeopardy. I am not saying attempt suicide because it will change your life. I am saying **don't** because you can change your life. God can change your life. Life is precious. Life is sacred. Life is our one opportunity to change anything and everything. People ask me if I could change what I did, if I could change the decision to attempt suicide. The thing I say most often is this: I would change my faith and by doing so, change myself. I will walk closer to God before I *have* to walk closer to God. I will love more, share more, and be a friend more. I will do everything I can differently, like show my feelings or open up. I will put away the merely happy face and learn to be joyful in who I am and what my circumstances are. I will be who I was made to be because I would not be here without some stronger force holding me here. And I am so glad that He did.

I hope that by reading this you find your joy. I hope that this inspires you to take a look at your life and the things that make you unique and find that you are not alone and that there is hope even when you cannot seem to find it. God is always by your side and even when you cannot hold on any longer, God is still holding you in His arms and He will not let His baby go. We often hear stories about mom's lifting cars to get to their children, or running through gunfire to save their kids. How much more will God do for you, His precious child? What more has He done?

Since this experience, things in my life have really changed. I know that things can change for everyone, but I hope that suicide is never an option for you or a family member because it changes everything. My dad always says, suicide is a permanent solution to a temporary problem. And it is so true! God will take that problem and change those circumstances; you just have to give Him a little time.

Dear God, thank You for always being here for me. Thank You for holding me and loving me when I felt no love and no hope. Please continue to look after me during my time of growth and struggle so that I may one day face another challenge and triumph knowing that You were the true Victor and I was just the vessel. Lord, although I am experiencing a lot of pain and tragedy right now, I know that You will always be by my side to hold me and help me. Lord, You are the light of the world and my Savior and Friend. Thank You for being all these things and for giving me the opportunity to see it for myself while I still have time on earth to see. Thank You, Friend. Amen.

CHAPTER 11

Lessons Learned

When I read over my daughter's words, and see how much she has changed from that time, I am so grateful to God. But all this did not happen overnight. We had to stop everything, and re-evaluate everything, and make some major changes. Even the smallest things in everyday life took on a new significance. We were fortunate to have some time before school started, and we found a counselor that we felt would be a good match for Erin. We rearranged our house, and put the medications in another place, at least for awhile. I stopped buying any medication in bulk.

We had some good laughs over it, too. After all, if you don't laugh, you'll cry, right? Every so often Erin would hint that she was feeling edgy and warn me with a wry smile that she was feeling suicidal again. "I got one word for you, kid," I'd say, "catheter." And we would bust up laughing. Sometimes Erin would ask for something, and if I seemed to be tending toward saying "no," she would look at me and say, "Mom, it's for my therapy."

People treated us differently, or at least I thought so. They didn't know how to ask about Erin, they didn't know what to say. Usually it was a half-hearted, "Are you guys alright?" and they always looked relieved when I just said, "Yes, fine." When you are in church leadership, as both my husband and I are, you tend to find yourself isolated. The very best friends were the ones who just loved on us, and let us pour out our hearts. I remember calling a great friend in Ohio, and she just let me talk. At the same time, she was in a crisis herself, so then I listened to her. Then we prayed together on the phone. It helped put it all in perspective, and made me realize that my problems, as severe as they were, were echoed in the lives of others.

Family members wanted to see Erin. Her grandparents were so anxious about her, and just wanted to hug her and make sure she was alright. Erin was uncomfortable with all this attention, and the initial contacts with others were sometimes awkward. We tried to keep things casual and keep life in a normal rhythm. Every so often, we scrape up enough money to go to the beach, and rent a big house at Topsail Island in North Carolina. In August we took our kids, all of them, including the three grandkids, off to the beach, and it was a great time. Erin and Beka found matching surfing shirts to go over their bathing suits. John-Mark and Josh, however, found some bright red ridiculous swimming trunks at a local souvenir shop, and putting them on stood outside on our back porch barbequing the supper, and frightening the neighbors (hey — we'll never see those people again, so don't judge). Patrick was the only one who couldn't make it, and when he saw the photos of his brothers, was thankful that he had dodged that bullet.

The lessons I have learned have been shattering yet life-giving, painful yet bringing the refreshing presence of the Lord. Many of them have been lessons re-learnt. Returning to the questions I had when I began this journey, I would say that none of us is healed yet. That won't happen until we all arrive at the Tree of Life. We all have trials and tribulations, we all have sins and faults that need forgiveness, and we all travel on our various journeys that God has set out before us. My wise husband says that we need some adversity so that we grow. The most illuminating moment in our lives after we understand the love of God is when we understand that we aren't in control. Christian maturity begins when a person realizes that only God is sovereign, and their best laid plans will always be subject to the pleasure of the Lord. A "normal" Christian is anyone who has surrendered to that, and you can find them in every country, every denomination, and in the most unlikely places. I once found a Christian sister working in one of those fancy lingerie stores in the mall. I had just had surgery to remove a suspicious lump on my breast, and she promised to pray for me, and was praising the Lord with me. I bought two brassieres from her.

Since we became a statistic, I have spent some major time reading about suicide (after all, that's what we educators do, we run to our experts and our reference books). The Center for Disease Control views suicide as a violent act, akin to domestic violence. You can read the frightening statistics online. Each year, in addition to the approximately 4,400 deaths among our youth from suicide, 149,000 are treated in our hospitals for self-inflicted wounds. For every suicide there are between 100 and 200 attempts. Boys are more likely to die from suicide, while girls more often attempt suicide but survive; also, girls are more likely to report an attempt than their male counterparts. Unfortunately, the statistics we have are all after the fact, and sometimes too late to help desperate children. And the numbers are on the rise.[3]

How do we stop this insidious killer? Experts in the field say there is no good test to predict a suicide attempt in the short run; it is very hard to know what is going on in someone's heart and mind. They do say not to ignore someone who is talking about suicide, especially if they have a specific plan and the means to carry it out. When these three aspects are all present – the idea of suicide, the specific plan and method of suicide, and the means to commit suicide – then the danger is much greater that an at-risk child will act on the impulse.[4] But what can we do?

We go to our knees. Our prayers become very clear, specific, and short when our kids are on the line. There is no "piling up phrases like the Gentiles" when the need is urgent and the stakes are high. Sometimes all you can do is cry "HELP!" And the best part is when we pray together. My husband and I prayed, in a deep way we hadn't in years. Friends prayed with me and for me. People came around me and lifted up words when I had none. There was no empty chattering, these were prayers that pronounced the assurances and promises of God to us; words of Scripture, words of faith. Prayer is intimacy with God, it is the most powerful weapon we have. Jesus told us to ask in His name, to ask with thanksgiving, to come persistently even when we see no progress, no outward change. God is always at work, and when we pray, He moves Heaven and earth aside to come to us. Psalm 18:1-19 (ESV) tells us:

> I love you, O LORD, my strength.
> The LORD is my rock and my fortress and my deliverer,
> My God, my rock, in whom I take refuge,
>> my shield, and the horn of my salvation, my stronghold.
> I call upon the LORD, who is worthy to be praised,
>> and I am saved from my enemies.
> The cords of death encompassed me;
>> the torrents of destruction assailed me;

the cords of Sheol entangled me;

the snares of death confronted me.

In my distress I called upon the LORD;

to my God I cried for help.

From his temple he heard my voice,

and my cry to him reached his ears.

Then the earth reeled and rocked;

the foundations also of the mountains trembled

and quaked, because he was angry.

Smoke went up from his nostrils,

and devouring fire from his mouth;

glowing coals flamed forth from him.

He bowed the heavens and came down;

thick darkness was under his feet.

He rode on a cherub and flew;

he came swiftly on the wings of the wind.

He made darkness his covering, his canopy around him,

thick clouds dark with water.

Out of the brightness before him

hailstones and coals of fire broke through his clouds.

The LORD also thundered in the heavens,

and the Most High uttered his voice,

hailstones and coals of fire.

And he sent out his arrows and scattered them;

he flashed forth lightnings and routed them.

Then the channels of the sea were seen,

and the foundations of the world were laid bare

at your rebuke O LORD,

at the blast of the breath of your nostrils.

He sent from on high, he took me;

he drew me out of many waters.

He rescued me from my strong enemy

and from those who hated me,

for they were too mighty for me.

They confronted me in the day of my calamity,

but the LORD was my support.

He brought me out into a broad place;

he rescued me, because he delighted in me.

This picture of God shows Him coming swiftly and powerfully to our rescue. It is as if God is saying, "Someone is touching **My** child, and I will act!" Pray to God; it always works. And if you can't find the words, open up the psalms and read them aloud. You will find words that fit your feelings exactly. God put those words there for you, centuries ago people blown along by the Holy Spirit wrote words to express their worship — and they experienced the whole range of human emotions just as we do. Their poetry can help us talk to God, to praise, even from the depths of despair, and to plead for our needs with the passion and honesty, for God will hear. "I love the LORD, because he hears my prayers and answers them, because he bends down and listens, I will pray as long as I breathe." Psalm 116:1,2 (NIV).

I learned to listen. A suicide attempt is a scream for help, and lots of times we don't listen until the scream comes. I prided myself on being very in touch with my kids' lives, but since I am analytical by nature I tend to hear things, file them away, and move on. Even if I have really heard them it may not seem to others that I have, and that is critical. In the busyness of life our frenzied pace can lead us to hurry and not take time. I have learned to take time to listen, to hear, and to let my kids know I have heard (this works with other people, too).

I have learned that we cannot ignore the warning signs. If a child or teen talks about suicide, we cannot write it off as nothing. It might be an angry over-reaction of the moment and it might be more serious. I have learned to ask about why they are saying it, and try to find out what the trigger is that has made the misery factor spike. And I have learned to get help. A third outside party who does not pass judgment on the child but can give the child a means of venting in a safe environment can help defuse the immediate pressure. Such a counselor can also assist parents in relating to their child and growing closer. We cannot solve all our children's problems; sometimes we need outside help, sometimes we need professional help. Mental illness is no less serious than cancer; we wouldn't try to heal cancer on our own, we would seek out medical advice. I have learned the value of Christian counselors.

I have learned again the value of an open home. We have always welcomed our kids' friends, hosting volleyball games and sleep overs and study sessions and sledding events on snow days. Sometimes we had kids just show up for dinner, and I always tried to make sure there was extra just in case. It helps me stay in touch with my kids and with their peers. We were considered a "safe house" by other parents, and we also networked with other parents where we knew our kids would be safe. It keeps the lines of communication open, so that when a child is at risk, there is a greater chance that someone will share the need.

Teens talk much more to their friends and peers than they do to their parents. It is a fact of life, and some of us parents may believe it is a result of the fall. However, this may be one place where the warning conversations about suicide take place, and how can a parent know this information? A good friend who hears a child talk about suicide may be willing to confide in trusted adults if they know us as compassionate and caring. I am not talking about being cool in their eyes. I am talking about the kind of adult that creates the aroma of security. If we are this kind of adult, kids may confide in us about their own problems and suicidal thoughts if they see us as a safe and trustworthy adult. If that happens, and we think the situation could be volatile, we need to get some help. Find a third party, a counselor or clergy or someone to intervene. We cannot let a child's secret threat to attempt suicide go unaddressed for fear we will be seen as an un-cool adult who betrays confidence. It is poor consolation to stand at the graveside of a boy or girl whose life was lost because of silence, and say that we were the cool adult who never gave their secret away.

I have learned we need layers of protection, and circles of community. One of the hallmarks of despair is being disconnected. Like the concentric circles on the surface of the water when we toss a pebble in, we all need circle upon circle of community. Faith and family, extended family, church and neighborhood, school and activities are some of the circles that surround our children. Our relationship with God should be at the center of our lives, but as one wise child said, "God doesn't have any skin on Him." God's love for us is a wonderful truth, but the only way to put flesh on that idea for our kids is to be His representative in their lives. We are the premier evangelists of our kids. Our mothers are the first to sing and speak to us the songs of Zion, the first kiss of love on our foreheads, the first to whisper hope in our ears, the first to share with us the breath of life, the first hand to lead us in the ways of truth, and the one heart on earth that is knit irrevocably to our souls. Our fathers are the first to show us love through strength and protection and provision mirroring the heart of God, the first to give us the approval for our achievements, the first whose judgment tempered with mercy illuminates grace. There is no such thing as a perfect mother or a perfect father, but if we as parents are following after God with all of our hearts He is always faithful to fill up the gaps in our parenting.

I have learned the value of belonging. Children need to know they are loved by their parents, and wanted, and important to them. They have to have a home place, a family where they know they belong, where they are cherished, and that place is where they are safe to be themselves. We parents are the first line of defense against this terrible killer, and it is in our power to impress on our children that they are a gift and a joy not only to us but to God and the world. We instill value and purpose in our children, and we declare to them from the day they are born that they are precious. Even when tough love forces us to create boundaries that cause angry reactions, they must know that love of their parents which guides them to Christ's unfailing love. Whatever problems or trauma our children may face, whether it be outside our home, at school, or through a divorce or death, if the anchor of a loving parent never changes, then the child is much more likely to weather any life storm. By doing this we not only give them a human home in our hearts, but we point them to the heart of God where their eternal home is. We have to love our kids, declare to them that they are loved, and we disable the most unholy lie that the enemy sends to their minds.

I have learned God uses other people. God works through us as parents, but He also uses grandparents, aunts and uncles, teachers, counselors, coaches and friends. Sometimes there are gaps in family or community circles due to death or divorce or change. God is able to fill those gaps in through faithful people in our circles. We are not in this alone. God brings people into our lives, and into the lives of our children who share the good news. For believers, it is support when we need it. For our kids, it is confirmation from other sources that repeat and bolster what we have said; sometimes it means more when it comes from another saint. And I believe that God honors His promise in Proverbs; the lessons we teach our kids, the training we pour into them they will not ultimately depart from it. It may take a while to get them back into the Kingdom, but they will not forget the truths they learned at their mother's knees and on their father's shoulders.

I have learned the value of a wider community. Our children need other places where they are welcomed and included and valued. One of our biggest blessings in our family has been grandparents. Our kids have had the love of grandparents and great-grandparents, have heard their stories and been brought with love into a wide family circle. They are tied generationally not only into the blood lines, but also into the heart lines of their grandparents. My parents and in-laws have given a wonderful legacy of roots to our children by hooking them into a branch of the family tree. They spend time with them, take them places, and have them come to visit. They teach them about cooking and farming and golf and crosswords; whatever they happen to love. Church is also a great place to find this. Kids who are also tied into a religious community that is caring reinforces their family ties. They may find wider communities on a sports team, an activity at school, band or choir, a club or a bowling league, art classes, scouts, or even a part time job or paper route. Any good program will boost the infrastructure of his or her security and understanding of his or her own worth as a person. Of course it is important to monitor these external communities and be present for these events. If we invest in our kids' activities — get involved and be supportive in their athletic and band and theater booster groups and parent-teacher groups, we have connections with teachers, coaches, and other parents. Parental presence and visibility is one of the most powerful supports and is also a deterrent to suicide and other threats to a child's wellbeing. A child's group of friends becomes more important to him or her on entering the teen years, and parents need to be aware of who those friends are. Peer groups can actually undermine and shred personal worth more effectively than anyone, and their importance in the child's life magnifies their impact.

It sounds absolutely basic, but we need to know where our children are at all times, whom they are with, and what they are doing. Neglecting to inform us of any one of these three elements cost my kids a week of their freedom. And my husband and I had a strict equal information for both parents rule. There was no playing one parent against the other in our household. Greg and I always talked to each other and made the kids check with both parents for permission to go out. It was not unknown that we would show up at an activity to be sure they were exactly where they said they would be. We also made a point of welcoming our children's friends into our home and getting to know them. Kids from the neighborhood and from school were invariably at our house for movies and popcorn, homemade cookies and home cooked dinners, sleepovers, and games of kick the can, volleyball, and dark tag. Of course, when there was a snow day, all the kids within walking distance found their way to our awesome hill for sledding, which was always followed by hot chocolate inside.

Technology is also an ever-expanding access point to our children; it requires careful monitoring of computers, cell phones, and media. The social networking websites came later in our family life, but when they started up I required my kids to use my e-mail address for their social networking. I saw every message that came through, hundreds per week. This is time consuming and challenging, but if it saves a child from suicide or drug abuse or assault or sexual exploitation it is well worth the time and trouble. In serious cases, access to mental health services and counseling increases a child's chances of avoiding this ultimate choice. Giving a child the skills to solve problems, to resolve conflicts with others and to find nonviolent means of handling disputes provides habits of right choices, instead of wrong ones. Finally, we teach our children to value life. God values life, that He is our Life-giver, that we are made in His image. Human beings are the crown of creation, we are the last and best creation of a loving God Who yearns jealously over the spirit He has caused to dwell in our flesh. We are infinitely valuable to God. These core Christian beliefs in the essential dignity and worth of human life as well as pro-life cultural values discourage suicide and support instincts for self-preservation.[5]

I have learned the value of instilling the idea of calling in our kids. What I mean is, part of our job as parents is to help our children discover their special abilities, their spiritual gifts, and their vocation in life. With five children, I can testify that every one is different and this is hard sometimes to discern. We often want our kids to follow in our footsteps, but they may not share our interests or our gifts. Give them a sense that God has a special plan for their lives, that He has designed them for a purpose, and that there is a future and a hope that includes being productive and satisfied in a calling. Giving them lots of things to try, then noticing and affirming where they excel in school and activities can be the encouragement they need to think creatively about using their strengths for a life's work. The conviction that they are needed in society can be a powerful motivator for study and pursuit of excellence, and also a deterrent to self-harm.

Parenting means putting our needs second to our kids. As a mother I was constantly setting aside needs and wants. If we didn't have money for everyone to go to the dentist, I brushed and flossed more and sent the kids. If there was a choice between my getting new shoes and the children getting them, the kids always got the shoes (I developed the fine art of making a pair of sneakers last at least three years!). But we cannot give to others if we are empty ourselves. Many of the lessons I learned or learned again were self-care lessons that enabled me more effectively to help Erin and my other children. What were those lessons?

I learned to use my weaponry. What is it that helped me through the darkest days? Prayer, Scripture, and music. I love to sing. I love all kinds of music, hymns and praise and worship music and rock and classical and Christmas music. I'll sing anything with a Jesus message. From years of musical training I have tons of hymns and songs memorized. Forcing myself to bring them out and dust them off and sing again helped me lift my eyes to Jesus. I played music on the stereo or in the car all the time. I sought out new songs and if I found one I loved that touched my heart, I bought the music and learned it. Then I would take it to church and sing it in the service. But that is just my weapon, my style of worship. You need to find your weaponry. A friend of mine is very athletic, a great runner. Her weaponry is doing eight miles at a stretch. Another friend of mine sews; she can whip out a formal dress in one day. You need to find something that turns the valve of your stress-o-meter and lets the steam out. It can be most anything, but combined with prayer and Scripture, there is nothing more powerful than your personal way of praising God and fighting the clouds of despair.

I also learned to keep my routines: schedules and meals and exercise and work. It's all too easy to sit around all day in your pajamas when something hits you hard. But getting up, getting coffee and having my devotions, stretching out and getting dressed, going to work, and going for regular walks — all these scheduled things in my life helped me not get sucked into the vortex of fear and grief.

I learned to keep serving. While I was hurting I still visited those who were sick. I still wrote for others, taught others. Sometimes it was teaching what I most needed to hear myself: God's grace and faithfulness and steadfast love and promises to never leave us nor forsake us. When asked to do a funeral, I obliged. Preaching resurrection from a position of powerlessness helped me focus on where the real power of our faith lies. I shared communion in the community of believers — that blessed meal of bread and wine — repeating the words of the Great Thanksgiving with awe as we lift our hearts and voices in the mystery of our faith: Christ has died, Christ is risen, Christ will come again.

I learned to go places, places I loved or places I'd never been before. I went with friends, with family, with church family. We would go to a museum, or a play at the amphitheater, or to a ballgame at the local park. Sometimes I would go alone. I would take a walk at a local park through the woods, or go to one of the many majestic overlooks where you can see the mountains rising above the New River, a vista that stretches beyond the furthest reach of vision, and seems to touch the sky and meet Heaven itself. I took my camera and put the pictures on my computer.

Another lesson I learned is that we all need a support group, some friends in Christ who will hold us up. This is hard for me because I am naturally a loner and an introvert. My favorite way to spend time is with a book, a cup of coffee, and a lot of solitude. But too much solitude can be a bad thing. God calls us into community. God calls us into relationship not only with Himself, but with others. The Christian life is not just one on one with God, but also a shared fellowship with every other person who names the name of Christ as Lord and Savior. While we have a huge family in faith, there should always be a few intimate prayer buddies to support us in our walk. Of course in the Christian family you have this intimate kind of support with each other. But when your family is under assault, it is wonderful to have some folks in the wider circle of the church to pray, to bring in some love and practical help. It is a mutual fellowship of praying for each other, and holding each other accountable, and bringing joy and blessed assurance to each other. I would go even further and say that every woman needs some girlfriends in Christ and every man needs some guys to hang out with in Christ. These are the people with whom we build strong intimate friendships and people with whom we can be ourselves. They communicate the love of Christ to us when we are unable to do it for ourselves. It is also imperative that the relationship be mutual; that way we can also pour this kind of grace on them when they go through the valley.

The most important thing I learned is that we cannot fail God. I do a lot of ministry, preaching and teaching and singing and occasionally writing articles, and all of a sudden I felt unworthy. How can I stand up and teach, how can I reach out to others, when I am a failure? But that is also a lie of the enemy. The thing that most qualifies us to minister to others is the fact that we have walked through the valley with Christ. It is not a failure when something bad happens; it is a chance to learn to give thanks in all circumstances, to let Christ stand in the gap for us. God's great strategy for spreading the Gospel of Christ is to use human beings; flawed, sinful, troubled human beings. We can be most effective for others when we are genuine, and nothing helps us connect with others such as shared sorrows. Trying to hide our warts just makes us appear phony. Every one of us has a ministry, every one of us has something to do for God, and every one of us has a story. Our stories, our times of trial, these are the things that make our witness effective. In the furnace of human tragedy Christ is there with us, where our faith is forged and made stronger. And that is when we are most useful for Christ.

This experience has given me opportunities to connect with people in a far deeper way than I would otherwise. People meet me, and they may assume (as many of us do) that someone in vocational ministry must, by definition, have it all together, or that we are too holy to have any practical use in this world. I make it a point when I meet someone not to tell them what I do for a living, because I want them to give me a chance as a person, and not write me off as a holy roller. But even if they do write me off initially, once I begin to share our story they give me another chance. I am not just one of those pie-in-the-sky religious fanatics who are living in a fantasy world of cotton candy bliss, I have been through the grinder and I know what real life troubles are like. That gives us a connection that we could not have shared otherwise. It also proves the power of the Gospel, because I, who have seen the harsher side of life, have come through by faith. God's faithfulness through our crisis validates our testimony to others. I am, of course, judicious in how and where I tell our story. I don't just blab it to everyone I meet. But when I see an opening, a place where hope can make a difference, I try to reach out with the comfort we have ourselves received from God.

In Ephesians 3 Paul promises to pray for the people, telling them that every family on earth is named by God. Still, with all the different precautions parents take, no matter how often we tell our kids we love them, no matter how often we check on them, no matter how conscientious we are, still the unthinkable can happen in *our* families, to *our* children. While we never fit the profile for being at risk, we still found ourselves a suicide statistic. In the end, the only thing to be said is that we live in a broken world, and the effects of sin still penetrate our families. Remember Job; was there anyone that was better at honoring God in his life, his business, his health, and his family? Yet he too saw the impact of evil in all these areas. God calls us to be in this world, but not of it. He promises vast spiritual resources to help us live out our faith in all of life. Why does He do this? Why does He allow evil in our lives? Why does He take us through the valley of the shadow of death? To love us, to give us more grace to meet greater need, to grow us spiritually, and to remind us that we are dependent on Him. When we walk through the valley with Him, we experience the vastness of His love for us, that love which is unsearchable; the depth, and breadth and width and length of God's compassion on His own.

I sometimes think about how life would be without Erin; what it would be like if she had succeeded, how empty our home would be without the light of her smile. I am eternally grateful to God that He spared us, but I know that there are thousands of families who have that empty place at the table, that Christmas stocking that will never again be placed by the fireside. There are people whose loved ones have survived the attempt, but are permanently disabled, or their health is impaired because of a suicide attempt. My prayers go out to you as I write this. My heart cries out to God for your sorrow, and the loneliness and the challenges of living a life forever changed by this new and difficult reality. Still I know, as sure as I know I am saved, that God's grace is always sufficient for our needs. You may think that my heart has not plumbed the depths of your grief, and you may be right. But the heart of God has certainly plumbed the depths of all grief. You can cast all your cares on God, because He cares about you.

CHAPTER 12

Permanent Solution

Suicide is not much mentioned in Scripture. You have Saul, falling on his sword at the end of I Samuel, and then you have the story of Judas Iscariot, the disciple of Jesus. Back in 2005 I wrote a lesson about the Passion of Jesus Christ from Matthew 26-27, a contrast of Peter's denial of Jesus and the Judas' betrayal of Him. The sins of these two men were very similar in intent. Judas conspired against Jesus and turned him over to the temple guard when He was alone and vulnerable, so they could arrest Jesus without fuss. Peter denied Jesus — denied he even knew Jesus — three times! Both men betrayed Jesus; both turned their hearts away from Jesus and stood against Him. When Judas realized what he had done — when he saw Jesus being put on trial, tortured, and condemned to death — Judas regretted his actions and repented; he threw the thirty silver coins, blood money for the Savior's life, back at the priests. Then he chose to end his life in bitterness and despair, hanging himself with a rope. Peter — also grieved by his own sin — chose to live on. He repented immediately and went out and wept, but even in despair the embers of hope were not completely quenched in his broken heart. Satan sifted him like wheat, but he carried on, through the crucifixion of the Christ he had confessed, through the death and burial of the one he had called "Lord," and to the resurrection, when he came and peered into the tomb to see Jesus' burial cloth and head napkin empty and folded on the stone ledge where Jesus had lain. What that first meeting with the risen Jesus must have been like for Peter! Did Peter look into Jesus' eyes, abashed? Did he hang back in the upper room while Thomas fell to his knees and cried, "My Lord and my God!"?

In John 21 we hear the rest of Peter's story. He gets up one morning and says, "I'm going fishing." Peter was out to sea in more than just one way. He wanted to rejoice in the resurrection of Jesus, but couldn't.

Six of his buddies are there and say, "Well go with you." So they head out to go fishing. This was so important, because it was an attempt to return to their former way of life, Peter's former vocation. For Peter it was a step backwards; he was judging himself. Now that Jesus was alive again, how could he, the one who denied Jesus, serve in the Kingdom? So he goes back to what he knows, his old job of fisherman. But as the seven men toil, once again, just like when Peter first met Jesus, they catch nothing. Jesus, resurrected Savior of the world, is there on the shore fixing them some breakfast, cooking some fish. They see Him on the beach, and He calls out to them, "Children, have you any fish?"

And they reply, "None."

"Throw your nets on the right side of the boat." Now every good fisherman knows that fish do not hide on one side of the boat, but the disciples listen to Jesus, throwing the nets over the right side of the boat. And just like when Jesus first called Peter, there is a miraculous catch of fish.

John shouts out, "It is the Lord!" As soon as he hears this, Peter, who has stripped for work, throws his outer garment on and dives into the sea to swim to Jesus. Isn't that interesting? Most people would not put extra clothes back *on* to swim, but I think Peter put his garment back on to cover himself; it was a psychological covering because he felt so exposed, felt so naked in his sin. I can just see him coming up out of the water, dripping with his heavy water-soaked clothes, coming right up to Jesus. He stands there looking at Jesus with no words to say, panting from the exertion of his swim to shore. Meanwhile, his buddies have brought the boat in, dragging the net full of fish that was too heavy for six men to haul in.

Jesus looks at Peter with compassion, and gives him something to do; something physical, something simple. "Bring some of the fish you have caught." And Peter, wanting so badly to get right with Jesus again and to be of service, and so eager to please, he goes over to that huge net bursting with 153 fish and singlehandedly hauls it over to Jesus. With super human strength Peter does what John and James and Andrew and Thomas and the other two guys could not do together.

But do you remember what Jesus was doing before the disciples recognized Him? He was grilling fish! He already had some fish! He didn't need any fish from Peter. But He gave Peter a job to do, something within his capacity, so that he knew he was still useful, that he could still be forgiven and brought back into the fold of God and work at a calling for Christ.

You know the rest of the story. Jesus invites them to have breakfast with Him, and then He sits with Peter and asks him, three times, "Simon, do you love me?" And three times Peter answers, "Yes, Lord, you know I love you." Three denials, three affirmations, and the forgiveness of the Savior floods into Peter's misery and reinstates him in grace.

Look at the end results of these two men: Judas killed himself in despair; Peter however, did not let despair win. Peter turned back to Christ; he chose to accept forgiveness from Jesus, and to live on, to be redeemed and welcomed back into the love of Christ! Peter's sin, his failure, his betrayal was not the end! To me, the greatest tragedy of Judas' story is that he could not believe that Jesus would forgive him, that God's grace could not cover even *this* sin, the sin of betrayal. Peter believed, and was restored. More than that, Peter became a great evangelist for Christ, and was useful once more to serve Christ. Peter knew then that God's forgiveness can cover anything. I have known this myself, and I know what it is like to stand dripping on the shore and look into the eyes of Jesus and hear Him say, "Elizabeth, do you love Me?" And I say, "Yes, Lord, You know I love You." Then He says, "Feed my sheep." Even when everything falls apart Christ can and does put it all back together, and we can again serve Him. No matter how far we fall, there is grace. I have seen God minister this to me, and I have seen Him minister this to my whole family. We not only are restored, our purpose and our ministry is also restored. God's always got a new Plan A.

On the Easter after Erin's suicide attempt I took this lesson out, dusted it off, and reused it for a Holy Week service of our local ministerial association. What new depths of meaning came out of it for me! After the presentation, Erin and Beka came to the podium and sang with me. It was a song of life, the life that is in Christ from the very inception of our salvation in Him. I think that was the first time I felt that I was coming up out of deep waters, and that *I* had a future and a hope. What a time of healing and joy!

Jesus Himself was tempted with suicide, when Satan told Him to throw Himself off the pinnacle of the Temple. Satan took Jesus to the seat of God's earthly power, the holy Temple of the Jews, and he quoted Scripture to try to convince Jesus to prove Himself and test God by arrogance and selfishness and disdain for His gift of humanity. Not only did Jesus refuse the temptation in that moment, but He also accepted His mission. He chose, not the path of suicide, but the much harder path of His ministry, that would culminate on a hard wooden cross. In this moment, as in so many others throughout the Gospels, Jesus chose the path to Golgotha, He affirmed His mission, He did not take the easy way out, but set His face firmly toward Jerusalem. Because our precious Lord Jesus Christ was committed to becoming our eternal Savior, we never again have to bear the heavy burdens of the lies of Satan, the burdens of fear, guilt, and sin, or face an eternity without God. Jesus made the way for us. "Therefore He is able to save completely those who come to God through Him, for He ever liveth to make intercession for them." (Hebrews 7:25 KJV). Salvation through Jesus Christ is our permanent solution. It is the only solution that is eternally guaranteed for life and joy and peace and paradise.

I have held this story on my heart for a long time. In all my journaling and teaching I have become increasingly convicted of the need to share the comfort that God has given us through our difficult time. Rebekah asked Erin's permission to share her story in a creative writing class at school. I thought Erin's story was somewhat unique, but it is not. In their own papers, Rebekah's classmates also shared problems just as devastating: stories of cutting, rape, assault, and other suicides. In a small class of students, there were many whose souls were wounded and they were asking critical questions because of life rending traumas as devastating as our own. People are crying out for hope.

The week after Erin's hospitalization I was called on to do a funeral service. One of the relatives at the funeral took me aside to tell me her daughter had attempted suicide also. Another woman I visit lost her daughter to suicide. Another dear sister had a brother who hanged himself. Yet another sister told me that her cousins, brothers, had committed suicide on separate occasions. One of the highest incidents of suicide is among our military returning from deployment in war zones. The tragedy of despair is all around us, suicide or attempted suicide has reached epidemic proportions, and not just among our youth.

Erin's life's verse has brought me much comfort over the last few years. Jeremiah wrote his prophecy to a people who had been defeated, deported, and displaced. They had seen their country fall to the Babylonians, and they had seen the temple of the Lord destroyed. But Jeremiah tells them to settle down in their new homes, to build, to plant, to marry and have families. Through Jeremiah God promises them that they will one day return to Jerusalem and rebuild the temple, and in the meantime they must have faith and live with hope. In a way, all Christians are exiles, living and building and planting with hope until we reach our new homeland. Our hope, our future, for this life and for eternity, is Christ.

Erin's Dad, my beloved husband Greg, was so right when he said that suicide is a permanent solution to what is always temporary problem. We get so focused on the immediate misery that we are fooled into thinking there is no way out, and to kill ourselves will put an end to the misery. This of course, is a lie. The misery of death is the misery of humanity, all the way since Eden. Death is, and was, God's way of protecting us from immortality in a sinful world, yet it should never be used as a quick out, cutting a life short at our own hands. We may think in a moment of depression or anger or humiliation that our life is over, but it is not. We are destined for something much greater, in this life and the next. Scripture tells us that while we are here we are being transformed into the likeness of Christ, day by day, from one degree of glory to another. This life is a journey of increasing glory. Scripture also tells us that there is even more glory to come: "When the perishable puts on the imperishable, and the mortal puts on immortality, then shall come to pass the saying that is written:

'Death is swallowed up in victory.'
'O death, where is your victory?
O grave where is your sting?"

The sting of death is sin and the power of sin is the law. But thanks be to God, Who gives us the victory through our Lord Jesus Christ." I Corinthians 15:54-57 (ESV). James O. Fraser said, "A Christian is immortal until his work on earth is done."[6] Therefore every day that we awaken in this world is another day God has given us, another day to work for Him. Obviously, we are not finished with all the good works He has prepared for us to walk in; obviously there is more yet to do. Therefore, we cannot believe the lie that we are useless for God; we cannot believe the lie that there is no future nor hope for us. Suicide is not the permanent solution to our problems, Jesus is the permanent solution. He is the answer to all of our problems. He understands and cares for us, even in the deepest pit, even in the face of the most desperate temptation.

Despair is the devil's ultimate weapon. It is the lie that hope is gone, is non-existent. It is the weight of misery that destroys our ability to lift our eyes to God. It blocks the road to grace, to forgiveness, to new life, to a future filled with the blessings of God. It makes us blind to the treasures of growing through the difficulties, and letting Christ refine our souls. And it cuts off our future. As we have shared our story with others, Erin and I have met so many families facing not only suicide, but cancer, and accidental deaths, cutting, anorexia, bulimia, and a host of other problems that have increased despair like darkness and have extinguished hope like a sputtering candle. II Corinthians 1:3,4 brings us a promise for these times: "Blessed be the God and Father of our LORD Jesus Christ, the Father of mercies and the God of all comfort, who comforts us in all our affliction, so that we may be able to comfort those who are in any affliction, with the comfort with which we ourselves are comforted by God." (ESV) All of us have received the comfort of God, the mercies of our dear Heavenly Father, from time to time. The purpose is always two-fold; one to comfort us, and the other to enable us to share God's comfort with others. We receive comfort from God, we are wrapped in His mercy and compassion, Whose heart knows and shares our every grief, Whose Son shared our sorrows and bore our iniquity. We are vessels of grace. Then, because we have experienced the healing power of His comfort, we are equipped to share that comfort with those who are hurting, and especially those who suffer with the same problems that we have come through. It is cyclical; what we have received we also can give. The world is waiting for hope, and we have the privilege and the responsibility to offer it. Hope that is shared is hope that grows. It is the candle that shines in the darkness of despair, and instead of being snuffed out, it lights another candle, then another, then another. Hope brings faith, and faith brings life.

So what is our new Plan A? Josh and his wife have moved to sunny Florida where he works with veterans. They both donate time and work and money and resources to the Wounded Warriors charity for returning servicemen who have been injured in serving their country. We miss seeing them and the grandkids as often as we did before.

Patrick graduated fromWest Virginia University. Now he is working hard in the real world, and breeds cocker spaniels on the side. He is also in in a band. John-Mark also went to *the* university, graduated *summa cum laude*, and now is in medical school there. Erin graduated high school with honors, also sang at her graduation, and went to a Christian university in Arkansas, to major in business. She spent a year back in West Virginia at one of our smaller universities, working on a certificate as a wedding and event planner, and competing in ballroom dance. She then returned to Harding University where she graduated. She has a job now in a local resort working as a catering manager. She is looking into graduate programs for Christian counselors and teaching, and her calling may lead her away from business. Rebekah went to our all-state choir (twice!) and starred in the school musical *You're A Good Man, Charlie Brown* as Lucy Van Pelt (not type casting, really). After graduation (where she also sang a solo) she followed her brothers to West Virginia University. Her experience with Erin's overdose has made her think of going into youth ministry, and she is majoring in social work.

Greg has taken on another church part-time, and he still works full time for Uncle Sam. As we enter these empty nester years, and are transitioning our children out of our home and into the adventure of their own lives, we are trying new things. We recently took a trip to Israel, and fulfilled a life-long dream to see the Holy Land. I have also gone back to school and begun graduate work in theology and ministry. After all, why not complicate middle age with the extra stress of academics? Greg is so supportive of my education; it's not nuclear physics, but he is all for it. When I come home from a long weekend of study in North Carolina the household chores are done, the lawn is mown, and there is often a vase of fresh flowers waiting for me when I walk in the door. For me, it is a huge blessing to be able, after thirty years of parenting, to pursue my own education again and prepare for the ministry God most assuredly has for me. As a dear friend in her seventies once told me, "You never retire in the Lord's work!"

Perhaps some of you who are reading this are walking a dark path, passing through the valley of the shadow of death. I understand now the imagery that David chose for this most famous psalm, Psalm 23, because when death darkens our door, it is like a shadow that casts its pall over our entire lives. We long to get out of the valley and back up to the mountaintop of joy, where we can breathe the free air and feel the light of God on our faces. And there is, God promises, always an end to the valley of the shadow; **it does not go on forever**. God, our Emmanuel, He is right there with us in the valley. He has passed through it with victory, and there is not a step on the path or a dark corner that He does not know. There is not one place in that deep valley that has not known the light of Christ's presence. So as we walk by faith, and not by sight, the Light of the World, our dear Lord Jesus, is guiding us and never leaving us alone. Even when we cannot feel His presence, we know by His promise that He is there all the time. Our Comforter, the Teacher, is whispering to us, "This is the way, walk in it," and giving us enough hope for the next minute, and the next, and the next. He is pouring the love of Christ into our hearts. He is praying for us and with us, with sighs too deep for words. And after we have been tested for awhile, we will begin to climb out of the valley with Christ, having the peaceful fruit of righteousness growing more deeply in our lives. There **is** a future and a hope. God always lavishes love and grace on us, and provides encouragement and friends along the way. Look around you for the comfort and support of your Christian family; look into the Bible for the words of life, pray to your gracious Heavenly Father, and use your God-given weapons to dispel the darkness.

What a great idea my daughter had, to end with a prayer. But as I edit this final page I have to share with you that we have gone down into another major valley. The pain is so great and so fresh, that I find myself looking for hope again, battling the despair. But as God has taken us through before, I wait in full expectation of His grace to again destroy, in another glorious victory, the problem that we face today. So as I pray for you, please pray for me:

Eternal and loving Father, I pray for each person reading this. I pray for Your comfort to flow to all of us, the peace that passes all understanding, and the assurance of Your steadfast and everlasting love. Lift our eyes to Christ, the One Who did not consider equality with God a thing to be grasped but emptied Himself, and was obedient to death — even death on a cross! — for our salvation. Let Your mercies flow to all of us, and let us be encouraged and built up by grace. Fill us with Your Holy Spirit, so whether we are struggling with problems or grief or loss, we rely on Your power. Whether we walk that difficult path ourselves or with others, let us be vessels of grace. I pray for hope, hope for today and hope for eternity. Let us feel the encircling of Your arms, the depth of Your unlimited love, the whisper of Your voice in our ear. And when we have passed through the valley of the shadow of death, give us strength and courage to declare Your grace to others, to reach out with helping hands as channels of Your comfort. And when You have brought us all through, let us join together in glory praising the name of the God Who carried us all along. In Christ's name, Amen.

ENDNOTES

[1] Keller, Helen

[2] Tozer, A. W., *The Attributes of God, Volume I*, 1997, Christian Publications, Camp Hill, Pennsylvania, 55.

[3] (Center for Disease Control and Prevention n.d.)

[4] Jacobs, Douglas G., M.D., editor. *The Harvard Medical School Guide to Suicide Assessment and Intervention*, 1999, Jossey-Bass Publishers, San Francisco, California, 4-51.

[5] Suicideology.org retrieved 2-10-2012; U.S. Public Health Service, 1999

[6] Crossman, Eileen Fraser, *Mountain Rain*, 1982, OMF Book, Harold Shaw Publishers, Wheaton, Illinois, 3.

CPSIA information can be obtained at www.ICGtesting.com
Printed in the USA
BVOW09s1123240214

345833BV00002B/3/P

9 781490 816197